ROUTLEDGE LIBRARY EDITIONS:
JUNG

Volume 5

UNDERSTANDING JUNG UNDERSTANDING YOURSELF

By the same author:

Dreams and the Search for Meaning. (1986) Methuen Haynes: Australia.

The Inner Man: Men, Myths and Dreams. (1993) Pan Macmillan: Australia.

Facing the Fifties: from Denial to Reflection. (2000) Allen & Unwin: Australia.

Beyond the Mist: What Irish Myths Can Teach Us About Ourselves. (2000) Victor Gollancz: London.

Looking Inwards. (2003) Penguin: Australia.

UNDERSTANDING JUNG
UNDERSTANDING YOURSELF

PETER O'CONNOR

Routledge
Taylor & Francis Group
LONDON AND NEW YORK

First published in 1985

This edition first published in 2015
by Routledge
27 Church Road, Hove BN3 2FA

and by Routledge
711 Third Avenue, New York, NY 10017

Routledge is an imprint of the Taylor & Francis Group, an informa business

British Library Cataloguing in Publication Data
A catalogue record for this book is available from the British Library

ISBN: 978-0-415-82179-7 (Set)
eISBN: 978-1-315-75425-3 (Set)
ISBN: 978-1-138-79007-0 (Volume 5)
eISBN: 978-1-315-76443-6 (Volume 5)
Pb ISBN: 978-1-138-79858-8 (Volume 5)

Publisher's Note
The publisher has gone to great lengths to ensure the quality of this reprint but points out that some imperfections in the original copies may be apparent.

Disclaimer
The publisher has made every effort to trace copyright holders and would welcome correspondence from those they have been unable to trace.

Understanding JUNG Understanding Yourself

Peter O'Connor

methuen

A METHUEN PAPERBACK

First published in 1985 by
Methuen Haynes
(an imprint of Methuen Australia Pty Ltd)
44 Waterloo Road, North Ryde 2113

First published in Great Britain in 1985 by
Methuen London Ltd.
11 New Fetter Lane, London EC4P 4EE.

National Library of Australia
Cataloguing-in-Publication data

O'Connor, Peter A., 1942-
Understanding Jung, understanding yourself.

Bibliography.
ISBN 0 454 00842 2.

1. Self-realization. I. Title.

158'.1

Reproduced, printed and bound in Great Britain by
Hazell Watson & Viney Limited,
Member of the BPCC Group,
Aylesbury, Bucks

Contents

TO FRIENDSHIP

Visita interiora terra rectificando
inuenies occultum lapidem.

Viridarium Chymicum, Stolcius, 1624

(Visit the inward parts of earth; by rectifying
thou shalt find the hidden stone.)

Preface

I first came across Jung's ideas in the very early 1960s, and I can remember the frustration and sense of awe that characterised my attempts to explore his theories. The few volumes of the *Collected Works* that I could lay my hands on seemed for the most part incomprehensible, and there existed little else in the way of books on Jung. I gradually searched out what was available in the way of introductory books, and two in particular were influential and important: Frieda Fordham's *An Introduction to Jung's Psychology* (Pelican, 1953) and Jolande Jacobi's *The Psychology of C. G. Jung* (Routledge & Kegan Paul, 1962). However, it was the publication in Switzerland of Jung's autobiography, *Memories, Dreams and Reflections* in 1962 (in England in 1963) that undoubtedly exerted a powerful effect on me and immeasurably strengthened my desire to explore Jung further. The publication of his *Man and His Symbols* in 1964 provided further impetus to this desire. This was followed by an exploration of the writing of Marie-Louise von Franz and James Hillman, both of whom have been through their writing a source of stimulation and learning.

Nevertheless, after twenty years of reading and reflecting on Jung, I was still struck by the fact that as a view of the world his writings were still relatively inaccessible. At the same time, paradoxically, the number of people wishing to study Jung seemed to me to be ever increasing. Thus upon my return to Australia from the United Kingdom in 1981, I began to prepare a series of introductory lectures on Jung for the lay person. I gave these lectures at the Council of Adult Education in Melbourne throughout 1982. Although many of the attenders had read Jung, few had had an opportunity of hearing formal lectures on Jungian psychology and of participating in discussion. Despite my own pessimism about the viability of lectures as a medium for exploring Jung, I was deeply rewarded by the gratitude, warmth and enthusiasm of the participants. The experience of most of the participants seemed to be that the level at which I pitched discussion of the theory and of its application to everyday life facilitated some integration of Jung's ideas. Prior to this it seemed that a gap had existed between Jung's theories and themselves as individuals; a gap partly due to the difficulty inherent in Jungian theory and in books on Jung.

Thus it became clear to me that there existed a need for a basic introductory book: a book that, like the lectures, and despite an acute awareness on my part of my own limitations in knowledge and understanding of Jung, could serve as an 'introduction' to 'introductory' books on Jung.

As we head towards the last decade of this century, I think that the increasing interest in Jung is no accident. Rather it reflects the fact that now the sexual revolution, to which Freud was a central figure, has passed, and the new anxiety is about the loss of meaning. It is the views of Carl Jung that speak so poignantly to this contemporary anxiety and indeed provide the most comprehensive and relevant understanding of it.

However, not unexpectedly, the loss of meaning

has resulted in a prolific market in meaning, and the anxiety I felt in lecturing on Jung and in simplifying his theories is that I may well trivialise them. This would render them 'marketable' in the market-place of instant meaning, a consequence that would do violence to the spirit of Jung and his theories. I hope that in this book I have avoided this, but at the same time provided an introductory book in every sense of the word. There is no pretence on my part that this book is a scholarly evaluation of Jung or Jungian theory. If the book serves its purpose, then it should leave the reader with a thirst and a sense of urgency in wanting to go beyond it and explore Jung further. With this goal in mind, I have provided a list of some suggested readings at the end of the book.

Apart from the obvious need for an intellectual introduction to Jung, I have formed the firm conviction that a sizeable percentage of people I have seen for psychotherapy have often had to reach a point of deep personal distress before they gained access to some thoughts, ideas and concepts that enabled them to make some sense of their experiences. Hence my additional hope is that this book might prove to be not just a book *about* psychology, but also a psychological book that facilitates the process of understanding by rendering some of the subjective experience of life objective: in other words, of simply bringing into consciousness, of making familiar and knowable, what was at another level of mind already known. In this sense the book will have failed if it merely imposes meaning and does not engage the reader in at least beginning to resurrect his or her own myth-making activity.

I want to take this opportunity firstly to thank the Council of Adult Education for the opportunity to give the lectures, and secondly to thank the participants for their most encouraging and stimulating discussion. I wish to place on record my gratitude to my colleagues at the Institute of Marital Studies at the Tavistock Centre, London, who could not have realised at the time what respect and re-affirmation of the unconscious mind they gave me.

My wife, Margaret, deserves my heartfelt thanks and respect, since, despite the ardours of the task, she continued to support and encourage me at times when I had grave doubts and conflict over preparing this book.

René Gordon also deserves my thanks, for in her capacity as a literary agent she maintained her belief in the manuscript.

I am also grateful and very appreciative of many individuals whom I have had the privilege of knowing in my capacity as a psychotherapist. The experience of these relationships and their role in the shaping of my understanding of Jung and myself could never be over-estimated. My specific gratitude is due to those individuals whose dreams or brief histories form part of the material of this book.

Finally, the task of transposing the lectures into typed form was carried out initially by Carolyn Holden and latterly by Marilyn Rowntree. I would like to record my thanks for the willingness with which they approached the work and the skill with which they executed it.

Melbourne, 1984 Peter A. O'Connor

Abbreviations

CW – C. G. Jung, *Collected Works,* 20 vols (see Suggestions for Further Reading, pp. 191-4, for publication details).

MDR – C. G. Jung, *Memories, Dreams and Reflections,* Routledge & Kegan Paul, 1963.

1. Carl Gustav Jung and the Jungian Perspective

Contemporary psychology seems to have become increasingly occupied with what is broadly termed the scientific model. As a direct consequence of this, a considerable amount of its focus has been on issues of proof and evidence for its assertions. In this sense psychology can be seen as reflecting the Western obsession with rationality and the denigration of the non-rational aspects of mind and being. This has inevitably altered the face and direction of psychology and, driven by the myth of logical positivism and quantification, it has moved away and out from psyche towards overt behaviour. At this manifest, observable level, the canons of scientific method can be met, variables operationalised, measured and – above all else – the fantasy of predictability and control can be achieved. Thus the increasing use of the term 'behavioural science' with its attendant passion for technology and measurement would seem to be a far more accurate description of much that passes as psychology today. That the inner world of man is complex and unpredictable is not a sufficient reason for psychologists to turn their backs on it in the defensive pursuit of certitude. Indeed, one can ask the question: what is psychology without a focus on the psyche itself?

Depth psychology, of which I regard Jung's theories as the most valuable and useful, is concerned with the inner world, and in this sense it is occupied with making objective or knowable to consciousness the subjective or inner world. It is its very occupation with the inner subjective world as opposed to the objective outer world that means the psychology depends very much on the psyche of the psychologist. In other words, as Jung himself said, the closer psychology reflects its subject-matter, the psyche, the more it merges with the psychologist himself. In so doing, it becomes like music or painting, an art form and always a subjective state.

Nowhere is this merging of psychology and psychologist more clearly seen than in the person of Carl Gustav Jung. In fact, his immense theoretical edifice can in the most basic of terms be seen as an attempt to reconcile and integrate the subjective and objective within himself. It seems to me ludicrous, particularly in this area of inner subjective-orientated or dynamic psychology, to separate the ideas out from the personality of the man to whom the ideas occurred. Hence the bulk of this first chapter will be concerned with Jung's personal background, followed by an attempt to distil from this the personal images and myths that may have been moving Carl Gustav Jung and propelling him to make sense of this inner experience. Finally, I will attempt to give a brief synopsis of the Jungian perspective that emerged from this complex fabric of Jung's personal life.

PERSONAL BACKGROUND

Carl Gustav Jung was born on 26 July 1875 in the small Swiss village of Kesswil on Lake Constance. He was the only surviving son of a Swiss Reformed Church pastor. Two brothers died in infancy, before Jung was born, and his only sister was born nine years later. His father, from Jung's own account in his autobiography, *Memories, Dreams and Reflections*, was kind, tolerant and liberal. However, he was also somewhat conventional and seemingly content to accept the religious belief systems in which he had been reared; unable, it seems, to answer the doubts and queries of his very gifted son. Jung actually describes his father as 'weak', and indeed goes so far as to say that, in childhood, he associated the word father with reliability, but also with powerlessness. (By way of contrast, Freud's father was described as strict and the undoubted authority in the home. It ought, therefore, not come as any surprise that Freudian psychology is a paternally-based psychology, or in Jungian terms a logos-based psychology, a masculine psychology, with persistent and consistent references to conscience, duty and fear of punishment as personified, for example, in castration anxieties.)

Jung, as Anthony Storr points out, belongs to that 'not inconsiderable group of creative people springing from families in which the mother is the more powerful and dynamic figure'.* Yet it appears that Jung's mother was, to say the least, a problematical figure for Jung. Sometimes she appeared to express conventional opinions, which another part of her then proceeded to contradict. When Jung was three years old, his mother is reported as having developed 'a nervous disorder', which required her to be hospitalised for several months. Jung later attributes this so-called 'nervous disorder' to difficulties in the marriage.

* Anthony Storr, *Jung*, edited by F. Kermode, Fontana Modern Masters, 1973, p. 7.

Jung's parents had marriage problems for as long as Jung could remember, and they slept in separate bedrooms. Jung shared a bedroom with his father, whom he described as being often irritable and difficult to get along with. Phillip Rieff, in fact, asserts that Jung's father 'had become a psychiatric case, complete with stays in an aslyum'.* Jung attributed his father's misery to the collapse of the Christian myth, and the inability of his father's belief system to sustain his being and give purpose to his life. However, Pastor Jung, being a conventional man, was caught by his own conventionality or conforming nature and was unable, or unwilling, either to reject his traditional Christian beliefs or to accept them – a classical bind that can be seen as producing neuroses.

In addition to Jung's father being a clergyman, eight of Jung's uncles were also parsons, so Jung as a boy must have spent a considerable time around black-frocked men. Brought up in such a household it was, it seems to me, inevitable that throughout his life Jung should have been preoccupied with questions of religion. By his own account, Jung was an introverted child who played by himself and in the attic of his house, where he took refuge. He had a mannikin, which he had carved from a piece of wood. This mannikin provided Jung with endless hours of ceremonies and rituals; secret pacts and miniature scrolls were hidden along with it in the attic.

When he was eleven, Jung began his secondary schooling at the gymnasium in Basel and, according to his autobiography, it was the beginning of a difficult

*Phillip Rieff, *The Triumph of the Therapeutic: uses of faith after Freud*, Harper & Row, 1966, p. 108.

period, involving firstly his neurotic fainting spells, following an incident where a fellow student had thrown him to the ground. From then on, for a period of six months, he lost consciousness whenever he wanted to escape going to school or doing his homework. Epilepsy was a rumoured diagnosis and, according to Jung, he overheard his father one day expressing concern about his son's future. Jung records that he heard his father saying: 'I have lost what little I had and what will become of the boy if he cannot earn his own living.'* Jung adds: 'I was thunderstruck. This was the collision with reality – why then I must get to work.' From that moment on, he says, he became a serious child and came to the realisation that he was to blame, not his schoolfriend who knocked him over or his parents. It seems that he, by his own account, overcompensated for his sense of 'rage against himself', by getting up regularly at 5 a.m. in order to study and sometimes working from 3 a.m. to 7 a.m. before going to school. On the other hand, his 'self cure' from the neurotic fainting spells also can be seen as foreshadowing one of the primary principles of Jungian psychotherapy; that is, bringing the patient back to reality and accepting the responsibility for herself or himself and not escaping this responsibility by a projection of blame onto others.

It seems that from then on all went fairly well with Jung's schooling, although he became aware, at an early age, about twelve, of two personalities within himself. The first, which he called his Number One personality, was a schoolboy who could not grasp

*C. G. Jung, *Memories, Dreams and Reflections,* Routledge & Kegan Paul, 1963, p. 43, hereafter cited as *MDR*.

algebra and was far from sure of himself. Indeed, one could see this as his ego-conscious personality. The other he termed his Number Two personality; 'a high authority, a man not to be trifled with, an old man who lived in the 18th Century'. In fact one could see this as his unconscious mind or personality. As Number One personality, Jung saw himself as 'a rather disagreeable and moderately gifted young man with vaulting ambition'. Number Two personality, on the other hand, he saw as 'having no definable character at all – born, living, dead, everything in one, a total vision of life'. This, in fact, could be seen as his inner self. Jung's autobiography records two or three other important inner events, either in the form of a vision or a dream, which he considers were powerful, formative experiences. He also records that the religious conflict persisted for him throughout his adolescence, and he says that he searched unsuccessfully through books for answers to his questions, since discussions with his father invariably ended unsatisfactorily. The picture that Jung draws of himself is that of a solitary, bookish, intellectual youth, puzzled by religious and philosophical questions. He says of these adolescent years:

More than ever I wanted someone to talk with, but nowhere did I find a point of contact; on the contrary, I sensed in others an estrangement, a distrust, and apprehension, which robbed me of speech. (*MDR* 71)

This predilection for the solitary, whether self-imposed or otherwise, can be seen as accounting for the fact that Jungian psychology is principally concerned not with the interpersonal relationships but with processes of growth, life and development *within* the individual psyche. It was this endeavour that became the focus of his Number Two personality. It is the events of this interior life that Jung mostly discusses about himself in his autobiography, *Memories, Dreams and Reflections.* In fact the period of his secondary and tertiary education is scarcely spoken of in his autobiography, except for references to interior events. Jung himself speaks strongly about the importance of these inner events when, in the Prologue to *Memories, Dreams and Reflections,* he says:

> Outward circumstances are no substitute for inner experience. Therefore my life has been singularly poor in outward happenings . . . I cannot tell much about them, for it would strike me as hollow and insubstantial. I can understand myself only in the light of inner happenings . . . it is these that make up the singularity of my life. (*MDR* 19)

He further states:

> Recollection of the outward events of my life has largely faded or disappeared. But my encounters with the 'other' reality, my bouts with the unconscious are indelibly engraved upon my memory. (*MDR* 18)

Thus it becomes clear why we know little of the facts of Jung's life from adolescence through to the completion of his medical training. We do know that two or three 'events' seem of paramount importance, when placed in the context of Jung's earlier life, in determining both the choice of career that Jung made and the development of his theories. These events could be seen as encounters with that 'other reality', the reality that became indelibly engraved upon Jung's memory.

The major one of these is, I believe, Jung's encounter with occult phenomena. I think a very substantial case can be built for seeing these encounters as fundamental to Jung's theories and views. A relatively recent book written by Stefanie Zunstein-Preiswerk entitled *C. G. Jung's Medium* has as one of its major themes the psychic or spiritualistic quality of the Jung family through several generations.* It is not only an attempt to capture Helene (Jung's first cousin, who performed mediumistic feats), but also an attempt to capture the psychological atmosphere that surrounded Jung during his student years. The evidence clearly indicates that Jung's involvement with occult phenomena coincided with his commencement of medical studies at Basel University in the summer of 1895, when Jung was almost twenty years of age. It also coincided with the death of his father some six months later, in January 1896. It is almost as if from the time his father took ill (according to the evidence, about twelve months prior to his death; that is, January 1895) Jung's mother began to express the other side of her personality, the side that Jung spoke of in the following terms:

I was sure that she consisted of two personalities, one innocuous and human, the other uncanny. This other emerged only now and then, but each time it was unexpected and frightening. She would then speak as

**C. G. Jung's Medium: Die Geschichte der Helly Preiswerk*, Kindler (Munich) 1975.

if talking to herself, but what she said was aimed at me and usually struck to the core of my being, so that I was stunned into silence. (*MDR* 58)

Further on he said:

There was an enormous difference between my mother's two personalities; that was why, as a child, I often had anxiety dreams about her. By day she was a loving mother, but at night she seemed uncanny. Then she was like one of the those seers who is at the same time a strange animal, like a priestess in a bear's cave. Archaic and ruthless; ruthless as truth and nature. (*MDR* 59-60)

In short, this 'other' and so-called different side of his mother's personality presumably was her unconscious side, if you like, her Number Two personality. I am suggesting that after years and years of habitually being repressed by her Number One side (that is, conventional personality), following the illness and subsequent death of her husband, the other side, the Number Two, began to assert itself, and this personality was strongly active in occult phenomena. Given a basic theoretical idea of Jung himself, it would seem that throughout his life he was influenced by, knew of and was linked to, his mother's unconscious mind, and hence his attraction to and fascination by occult phenomena was inevitable.

In the Swiss (1962) edition of *Memories, Dreams and Reflections* Jung says:

My mother often told me how she used to sit behind her

father when he was writing his sermons. He could not bear it that, while he was concentrating, spirits went past behind his back and disturbed him. When a living person sat behind him the spirits were scared off.*

This small quote reveals the fact, a fact explicated by Frau Zunstein-Preiswerk's book, that Jung grew up in an atmosphere in which occult phenomena and mediumistic activity were commonplace. Indeed, Jung says as much in his autobiography, when referring to an occult book he read during his student years. According to Jung, the phenomena described were: 'In principle much the same as the stories I had heard again and again in the country since my earliest childhood' (*MDR* 102).

It further seems that table-turning and seances had become the vogue in Basel, as elsewhere in Europe at the end of the last century. Just as Freud's basic ideas can be placed against sexual repression and attitudes towards children of Victorian Vienna it seems equally plausible to place Jung's basic ideas against the spiritualism of the 1890s. A most esteemed scholar, Henri Ellenberger, in a book entitled *The Discovery of the Unconscious,* goes so far as to state:

The germinal cell of Jung's analytical psychology is to be found in his discussions of the Zofingia Students Association [a Swiss student society] and in his experiments with his young medium cousin Helene Preiswerk.†

* Quoted by James Hillman, 'Some Early Background to Jung's Ideas', *Spring: an annual of archetypal psychology and Jungian thought,* Spring Publications, 1976.
†Allen Lane, 1970, p. 687.

Jung himself asserts a similar view when he states:

> This idea of the independence of the unconscious, which distinguishes my views so radically from those of Freud, came to me as far back as 1902 when I was engaged in studying the psychic history of a young girl somnambulist.*

Jung's first recorded experience of a seance was on an evening in June 1895, when he was nineteen, during which the cousin previously mentioned, Helene Preiswerk, personified a number of deceased family members. The seances appeared to have continued intermittently over a period of four years, and they were mainly confined to the family circle. Jung appears to have been particularly fascinated by the fact that, quite contrary to her normal waking state, one of the voices that Helene Preiswerk spoke in during the seance was in perfect High German instead of her customary Basel dialect. This young cousin's activity then became the focus of Jung's medical dissertation in 1902. Thus, before he began his active career as a psychiatrist in 1900, bearing in mind that Jung's original career choice was to be an archeologist, he had already developed quite definite ideas about psychology. Two things in particular seem to have attracted his attention with respect to Helene the medium. One was her ability, when in a mediumistic state, to accomplish performances that were far superior to those she was capable of in her conscious state. The other was the contrast between the major personality

*C. G. Jung, *Two Essays on Analytical Psychology,* volume 7 of *Collected Works,* p. 123, hereinafter cited as *CW.*

evoked during the mediumistic state, who was serious, poised, thoughtful and spoke in High German, compared to the medium's unbalanced habitual or outer personality. Jung concluded that the mediumistic personality was none other than the adult personality of the girl that was in the process of elaboration in her unconscious and that the mediumistic career was a means that the unconscious had utilised to express itself.

Herein lies the seeds of Jung's major theoretical ideas of individuation, along with the seeds of projection and its role in integration. He had learnt that parts of the unconscious mind could be split off (the essence of his later development of the idea of autonomous complexes) and take on the appearance of a human personality. However, more importantly, I feel that Jung learned from these mediumistic activities, along with one or two other seemingly inexplicable events, such as a table-splitting and a knife-shattering into several pieces (both events had no known external cause and both occurred around this same period), that the world of the unconscious consisted of far more than simply repressed material from consciousness, which was Freud's assumption. From an early age and particularly during these student years, Jung must have been heavily influenced by such occult phenomenon in such a manner as to confirm for him the reality of the psyche and its tendency to want to be expressed (that is, become conscious), in addition to it being simply composed of repressed material from consciousness. In short, the unconscious mind existed in its own right. The question then is not whether Jung believed in such occult phenomena or not, but rather to view experiences as having confirmed for him psychic reality – a reality that he spent his entire professional life exploring and trying to understand.

When these experiences are put alongside the religious conflict and disappointment, or rather disillusion with his father, then one can begin to construct a picture of what myth moved Jung. We know for fact that he perceived the Christian myth (and by myth I mean that image or set of images that give a meaning to life, that endow it with purpose and order) was no longer therapeutic (that is, able to sustain a person's sense of being). He had attributed his father's miserableness to its failure. From the beginning to the end, Jung's life can be seen as a record of an heroic struggle to find himself a personal myth by which he could live, free of the Christian myth that had failed to give his father a workable sense of well-being and purpose. But it is also clear that the myth, the struggle to make sense and order of his experience, had to be about the inner world, the world that was first awakened for him via dreams and the occult phenomena that his mother introduced and exposed him to. This myth, as we shall come to see, is primarily concerned with the reconciliation of opposites within himself. These opposites can be most clearly seen as the opposites of the objective and subjective worlds personified in his Number One and Number Two personalities; his father as a Number One personality and his mother as Number Two. Later, in his medical studies, Jung came across the psychiatric text by Richard Krafft-Ebbing, was immediately attracted to it and, to the annoyance of some of his lecturers and professors, elected to take up psychiatry.

Given his personal history, it must have seemed to Jung that psychiatry might fulfil his need to reconcile the opposites within himself, the Number One and Number Two personalities, the rational with the irrational, the objective with the subjective. It is this reconciliation of the opposites within that forms the central theme of Jungian theory. It is no accident therefore that he chose psychology, no accident that he developed the theories that he did, indeed such 'accidents' are simply the overt manifestation of the unconscious mind at work and the unceasing process of individuation.

2. The Nature and Structure of the Psyche

Part I: The Archetypes and the Collective Unconscious

In setting out to describe the life of the psyche and its processes, one can proceed from three viewpoints. The first of these is the viewpoint of its structural aspects (that is, what is seen or regarded as composing the psyche). Secondly, it can be seen from the standpoint of how and in what manner it functions (that is, from a functional viewpoint, which necessitates a discussion of the sources of energy, the distribution of the energy and the various relationships within the psyche between its structural parts). And, thirdly, it can be seen from the standpoint of its contents (that is, what makes up the structures and how they manifest themselves in everyday life). I shall deal firstly with the structural aspects, although this will, of necessity, include some discussion of the other two viewpoints. The later chapters, whilst still referring to structures, will increasingly focus upon the content of the psyche and its ramifications and applications to everyday life.

In essence, what I was endeavouring to get across in the previous chapter was that in the realm of psychology, where the subject-matter is subjective, one cannot separate the theory that has developed, or is explicated, from the personality of the individual who has developed it. Thus I tried to establish that Jung was no exception in this respect, and that it was no accident that he developed the theories he did with the underlying leitmotiv of reconciliation of the opposites. I tried to show that spiritualism and occult phenomena, so very prevalent in late nineteenth-century Europe, and specifically so in Jung's mother's circle of relatives, had established in Jung's mind the indisputable reality of the unconscious. At the same time, this distinguished Jung from Freud, as the latter regarded the unconscious mind as being solely composed of material pushed out of, or (in technical terms) repressed, from consciousness. The experience of seances, mediums, table-turnings, knife-shattering, table-splitting, etc., merely afforded Jung with ongoing confirmation of autonomous psychic activity and attested to the validity of the unconscious mind being more than merely a receptacle of unacceptable material from consciousness.

It was the further experience as a psychiatrist working in the Burghölzli Psychiatric Hospital that formed the raw data of Jung's development of the concept of the collective unconscious and the archetypes. His career as a psychiatrist began in 1900, coincidentally the year that Freud published his momentous study entitled *The Interpretation of Dreams*. One of the fundamental differences in experience between Freud and Jung lies in this period of Jung's professional work. He, unlike Freud, worked in what was then called a lunatic asylum with psychotic patients who, in the main, were deemed to be suffering from what was then called dementia praecox and is now known as schizophrenia. It was through his painstaking and diligent studies and investigations of psychotic patients that Jung came to realise that much of their delusional material could not be explained or derived from the patients' personal life or biography. In a neurosis, which was the form of personality disturbance mostly seen by Freud, the personalistic content, that is, the nature of the symptoms and their manifestations, can in the main be explained by resorting to the individual's biographical data. But in schizophrenia Jung discovered that personalistic causality failed to explain the peculiar ideas of schizophrenic patients.

This delusional material, or contents of the mind, seemed to Jung to be coming from a spot in the psyche that had never been conscious and not simply from material that had been repressed out of consciousness. Jung provided many classic examples of this hypothesis. One is from a so-called paranoid schizophrenic, who one day took Jung to the window, pointed up at the sun, and told Jung that if he was to look at the sun with his eyes half closed he would be able to see the phallus of the sun. If he was then to move his head from side to side, said the patient, he would see the sun's phallus move too. That was the origin of the wind, said the patient.

Some years later Jung came across a book written by Albrecht Deiterich containing a Greek text thought to be a liturgy of the cult of Mithras, a deity who was originally worshipped by the Hindus and Persians and later became popular in Rome. In reading the text, Jung came across a vision that exactly paralleled that of his patient. The schizophrenic who originally told Jung of the vision was a clerk of no high degree of education or culture. Moreover, the book in which Jung discovered the exact parallel vision had *not* been published at the time that the patient spoke with Jung, and therefore Jung concluded he could not have known of such material consciously. From this and other similar experiences with schizophrenics, Jung concluded that there was a myth-creating level of mind, common to both psychotics and normals and common also to people of different times and different cultures. This level of mind he came to call the 'collective unconscious'. Such myth-making activity is like a primitive form of science, purporting to account for the facts of the world as they appeared to pre-scientific man. Myths tend to order experience and make it more coherent for us. In schizophrenia, with the deterioration or suspension of rational ego-conscious activity, this primitive myth-making process is simply rendered visible.

Every person, according to the Jungian viewpoint, needs a myth to live by, and if he or she does not appear to possess one, she or he is either unconscious of it or else very badly alienated from the roots of his or her being, a state that Jung observed in his father and the failure of the Christian myth and a state that one can observe all too frequently in contemporary society. What is not generally appreciated is that Jung came to the conclusion that everyone possesses a 'delusional system', although he did not use that exact terminology. However, despite the early publication of his book on dementia praecox, in which some of these ideas were put forward, it was not really until 1909, during a trip to the USA with Sigmund Freud, that Jung seriously began to formulate the hypotheses of the collective unconscious and the world of archetypes.

According to Jung, the trip to the USA began in Bremen in 1909 and lasted seven weeks, during which time Freud and Jung analysed each other's dreams. One of these dreams, Jung declared, led him for the first time to the concept of the collective unconscious and thus formed a prelude to his book originally published as *The Psychology of the Unconscious* and later in the revised edition as *Symbols of Transformation*, now published in the *Collected Works* as volume 5. Here then is the dream that Jung had:

I was in a house I did not know, which had two storeys. It was 'my house'. I found myself in the upper storey where there was a kind of salon furnished with fine old pieces in Rococo style. On the walls hung a number of precious old paintings. I wondered that this should be my house and thought 'not bad'. But then it occurred to me that I did not know what the lower floor looked like. Descending the stairs I reached the ground floor. There everything was much older, and I realised that this part of the house must date from about the 15th or 16th Century. The furnishings were medieval; the floors were red brick. Everywhere it was rather dark. I went from one room to another, thinking 'now I really must explore the whole house'. I came upon a heavy door, and opened it. Beyond it, I discovered a stone stairway that led down into the cellar. Descending again, I found myself in a beautifully vaulted room which looked exceedingly ancient. Examining the walls, I discovered layers of brick among the ordinary stone blocks and chips of brick in the mortar. As soon as I saw this I knew that the walls dated from Roman times. My interest by now was intense. I looked more closely at the floor. It was a stone slab and in one of these I discovered a ring. When I pulled it the stone slab lifted and again I saw a stairway of narrow stone steps leading down into the depths. These, too, I descended, and entered a low cave cut into the rock. Thick dust lay on the floor, and in the dust were scattered bones and broken pottery, like remains of a primitive culture. I discovered two human skulls, obviously very old and half disintegrated. Then I awoke. (*MDR* 155)

In discussing this dream with Freud, Freud insisted that the skulls denoted a death wish. Jung, despite his resistance to this interpretation, suggested in turn that it might have been his wife and mother-in-law. For Jung, as we will discover, a dream is not something to which we apply a set of dogmatic fixed interpretations, which is what Freud did and indeed some Freudians tend to do, but rather that the dream is best seen as a kind of text not understood, like a Sanskrit or Latin text, which needs to be deciphered. Jung rejects the Freudian idea that a dream is a clever distortion disguising the original figure and instead sees the dream as a language that we do not understand. Jung held that: 'The dream is the whole thing and if you think there is something behind it or that the dream has concealed something, there is no question but that you simply do not understand it.'*

Jung took this approach to his own superbly rich dream which we have just read, an approach he often designated as that of a philologist, applying the logical principle of amplification. Such an approach yielded for Jung the hypothesis of the collective unconscious; he

* *Analytical Psychology: its theory and practice*, Routledge & Kegan Paul, 1968, p. 92.

saw the house in this dream as an image of the psyche with consciousness being represented by the salon on the first floor, the ground floor for the first level of consciousness, and the deeper he went as being more alien, until finally the long uninhabited prehistoric cave, which he saw as signifying past times and past stages of consciousness. Thus the unconscious was seen to have both a personal and impersonal or collective aspect. However, to attempt to actually define the collective unconscious is to attempt the impossible, for we have no knowledge either of its boundaries or its true nature; all we can do is observe its manifestations. Jung laid considerable stress upon the universal character of the collective unconscious, for example:

> It has contents that are more or less the same everywhere and in all individuals. It is, in other words, identical in all men and thus constitutes a common psychic substrata of a suprapersonal nature which is present in every one of us. (*CW* 9:1:4)

That is, the collective unconscious is not a personal acquisition. The mind, through its physical counterpart the brain, has inherited characteristics or innate predispositions with which to respond to life's experiences. In short, they are a pattern of apprehending life's major events. Through the collective unconscious, each individual is linked not only with his own past, but the past of the species. In this way, Jung's concept of the collective unconscious places the psyche within the evolutionary process. It can also be seen as a reservoir of latent images, which Jung called primordal images, simply meaning 'first' or 'original'.

In this sense the hypothesis of the collective unconscious links to Jung's dream of the skull in the prehistoric cave. It is as if below the salon in each of us are layers and layers of consciousness, the most original being the collective unconscious. Man, it can be argued, inherits these primordial or original images from his ancestoral past, but they are not specific images as such, not the specific image of his long-lost great-great-great-grandfather, but rather predispositions or potentialities for experiencing and responding to the world. I see them as closely akin to such innate behaviour patterns in animals, like migratory habits in birds or the incredible, complicated patterns of bees or wasps. While the specific place, etc., of migration for birds may vary, the innate migratory behaviour pattern does not. This is, I believe, what the collective unconscious in the simplest and clearest terms is about. That is, a substrata level of psychic activity that is to do with inherited predispositions to act or react in certain ways to certain life situations.

These innate behavioural patterns are what Jung has termed archetypes, which simply means an original model. A synonym of archetype is prototype. Of the archetypes Jung wrote the following:

There are as many archetypes as there are typical situations in life. The endless repetition has engraved these experiences into our psychic constitution, not in the forms of images, filled with content, but at first only as forms without content representing merely the possibility of a certain type of perception or action. (*CW* 9:1:48)

It is far too simplistic to assume that we have inherited a series of specific images. Archetypes are simply the predisposition to act, the mould, if you like, into which we pour specific images from life's experiences. In summary, then, archetypes are the tendency, one might even say the necessity, to apprehend and experience life in a manner conditioned by the past history of mankind, in this sense they are pre-existent forms of apprehension. As Jung said: 'Just as instincts compel man to conduct a life that is specifically human, so the archetypes compel intuition and apprehension to form specifically human patterns'.* Archetypal images are the symbolic representation of the archetypes or these primordial patterns or modes of pre-existent apprehension. The archetype is the mould; the actual manifestation to consciousness of the mould is the image. All that is inherited is the predisposition, not an idea, a predisposition to create significant images or myths out of the so-called common stuff of life. Hence the images tend to represent to consciousness innate predispositions for responding to typical human situations, such as birth, death, separation from parents, relationship to the opposite sex, etc.

Despite Jung's pessimistic view that 'not even our thoughts can clearly grasp the archetypes, because it never invented them', several recurring figures or archetypal images have been isolated, and these are known, primarily via analysis, to recur in dreams and fantasy series, which relate to some of the typical events for which we have such innate predispositions or pre-existing forms of apprehension. These figures

*'Instinct and Unconscious', *CW* 8:133.

can be seen as personifications of these innate predispositions and can be correlated with historical parallels and myths from all over the world; hence establishing the universality of the collective unconscious.

The major archetypal images described by Jung are the persona, the shadow, the anima, animus, wise old man, Magna Mater or great mother, miraculous child, the hero/saviour and finally the Self. In addition, there are a host of what could be called or termed archetypal objects, and these again can be seen as presenting to consciousness certain collective unconscious contents or themes (that is, archetypes). The major object, and perhaps one of the oldest, and most universally known to mankind is the mandala; others are trees, snakes, the sun, the moon, fish, birds, the sea, ships, the mountains, various reptiles, etc. Each rich and belonging to a mythological context.

In the remaining section of this chapter I would like to concentrate on some of the basic archetypal images that clearly belong to the collective unconscious and tend to have little in the way of personal meaning, such as the shadow, anima, animus and the persona have.

WISE OLD MAN

In dreams and visions, mythology and folklore, religion, esoteric cults, etc., there tends to be, almost without exception, a figure most conveniently subsumed under the title of the Wise Old Man. He takes many shapes in the collective unconscious, such as God, prophet, sage, law-giver, king, counsellor, philosopher, priest, professor, judge, doctor, alchemist, medicine man, sorcerer, wizard, etc. The Wise Old Man is the embodiment of the age-old experience, wisdom. Invariably the image gets projected onto figures in the outside world. Historically, such persons as Confucius, Aristotle, Marx and Jung are typical recipients of such projections of the Wise Old Man archetype. This archetypal image, like all archetypal images, has a series of consistent themes that are involved with it. The major ones of these are the great work, the theme of the discovery of the hidden treasure of wisdom, the acquisition of the knowledge that can miraculously transform us, the theme of the possession of a secret, or the secret of learning itself, wisdom and insight.

In short, as Jung once declared, the Wise Old Man image is to do with a search for meaning. At the personal level, the Wise Old Man can have the unfortunate effect, if not handled adequately, of resulting in a stultifying master/disciple relationship in which the 'master', if he accepts the projection of the Wise Old Man, feels compelled to live up to the image of an all-knowing, omniscient being. The disciple, instead of dealing with life himself, seeks out a parasitical existence, often made up on the one hand of uncritical acceptance of all the master does and says, and on the other of petty quarrels with fellow-worshippers and disciples. Several of the present-day Eastern cults and associated gurus and ashrams reflect, I believe, exactly this phenomena. Often with the absurd game being played within them of disciples being competitive over who is in fact the most spiritual! Such absurdity can only reflect an unfortunate aberrant form of the projection of the Wise Old Man.

On the positive side, projection of the Wise Old Man can be a valuable stage in psychological growth, so long as it is a stage and not a stagnation offering an analgesic against pursuing the meaning of life for oneself. If the recipient of the projection is a truly wise teacher, he enables the disciple or follower to see that such dependency in the long run is a little absurd and counterproductive. But successful transition depends on the maturity of the teacher. Psychotherapy, I believe, is a contemporary situation in which the dangers of the Wise Old Man archetype are rampant in so far as not only is the therapist vulnerable to such projection, but also the very nature of this work to do with insight, making him vulnerable to believing it about himself! Such a situation of identifying with the archetype, whether it be the Wise Old Man or any other archetypal images, is a perilous situation. Jung often referred to Nietzsche's invasion by the figure Zarathustra as a classic example of invasion by an identification within consciousness of the Wise Old Man. Jung himself must have had to exercise, it seems to me, enormous discipline not to have fallen prey to such projections himself, since he was not infrequently referred to consciously as the Wise Old Man of Zürich.

The way in which one handles archetypal images is to recognise the figure for what it is and to maintain a position of consciousness with respect to it. Give it attention, as Jung did, firstly with Elijah, then Philemon, two archetypal figures that he formed a working relationship with, but still maintaining one's conscious viewpoint. The goal is not to fall into unconsciousness (that is, madness), but to integrate and bring unconscious material into consciousness. That is, to maintain one's critical faculties and to differentiate between the image and oneself. Invasion by the Wise Old Man can be seen as the source behind the present-day cavalcade of self-appointed gurus, whether they be psychotherapeutic, philosophical or religious, who seem to be regularly invading the shores of our country just as frequently as they invade the shores of our consciousness.

MAGNA MATER

The Wise Old Man can be considered as being predominantly an archetypal image in the male psychology. Although, as will become apparent later, it can also appear as an image as part of a woman's animus or masculine side. The corresponding figure in a woman's psychology to the Wise Old Man is what has been termed the Magna Mater or Great Mother. In mythology, folklore and religion the Great Mother has played a powerful and continuous role from the earliest times. She has appeared under many mythological names, for example Ishtar of Babylon, Isis of Egypt and Demeter of Greece. She is also seen in many guises throughout mythology. She is the maiden, earth mother (Demeter), queen of the underworld (Persephone), goddess of love (Aphrodite), the goddess of marriage (Hera), the goddess of agriculture, and the goddess of the moon, etc., etc.

In short, the archetypal theme personified in these images of Magna Mater are the recurring themes of death and rebirth. Sometimes this rebirth can refer to spiritual rebirth, and the Magna Mater can be concerned with mystical and esoteric secrets whereby she can become the recipient of some powerful projections being seen as the source of all love. If a woman is inflated or possessed by this figure from the collective unconscious, she can come to believe herself to be endowed with an infinite capacity for love and understanding, of helping and protecting, and will wear herself out in the service of others. She can also destructively insist that all who come within her circle are her 'children' and therefore helpless and dependent on her in some way. This can be seen as a similar aberrant version of the master/disciple relationship.

This subtle tyranny of the woman possessed by the Magna Mater can demoralise, destroy and devour the personality of the individual who is locked into it. Often such individuals are found in various religious and esoteric cults. Although it is also valid to point out that just as a male psychotherapist is vulnerable to the Wise Old Man projection and indeed ego-identifying with it, I firmly believe that female counsellors and social workers are equally vulnerable to the invasion by the Magna Mater or Great Mother archetype. Obvious signs of this can be the failure by counsellors or social workers to establish appropriate boundaries around their professional work, and also the tendency to maintain clients in very vulnerable dependent relationships. In short, the effect of an invasion by the Magna Mater in a woman counsellor, or women in general for that matter, is to reduce those around her to an infantile and helpless position.

Where a woman can effect a positive working and conscious relationship with this archetypal image, then she is capable of extraordinary activity. The most conspicuous contemporary example of such a woman, to my mind, is the Nobel Prize winner Mother Teresa of the House of Dying in Calcutta. Historically, Queen

Victoria could be considered as an example of such a person.

THE MIRACULOUS CHILD

This image, often appearing in dreams as a gifted child, is the symbol of new possibility, of growth, of the new attempt, of the joyous renewal of life, of the vision of a new beginning. In the negative version we have such figures as Peter Pan or the child who never grows up, although always behind such a child image is the possibility of growth and renewal.

HERO/SAVIOUR

As with other archetypal images, the hero/saviour has a characteristic archetypal theme of which the hero/saviour figure is a personification. The theme is usually around such issues as the quest, deliverance, the discovery, the great deed. Mythologically, King Arthur personifies such a hero, Jason and the Argonauts is another, Orpheus and Ulysses are classical Greek hero-figures. Christ is, of course, an archetypal image of the saviour, and Mahatma Gandhi is a relatively recent example of such a hero/saviour figure.

CONCLUSION

In addition to the archetypal images in personified form, there also exist archetypal objects of which the major ones are such objects as a tree, snake, etc., and finally the mandala, which we shall discuss in detail later on in this book. Archetypal images hold out the great possibility of making conscious certain deeply held and felt unconscious forces. In this way, they further the psychological evolution of Self and thereby the psychological evolution of mankind. In the image form some contact can be made with archetypal forces, and man can take one small step toward self-realisation.

3. The Nature and Structure of the Psyche

Part II: Personal Unconscious

The central or underlying theme of the previous two chapters has been that Jung did not arrive at his understanding of the human psyche by accident. Indeed, as I have attempted to demonstrate, his early childhood experiences and later acquaintance with occult phenomena and his early experiences with schizophrenics all led Jung to the firm conclusion that the unconscious mind exists in its own right and often functions quite autonomously from the conscious mind. In the previous chapter I developed the specific idea that Jung's experience with psychotic patients, as opposed to Freud's with neurotics, had led Jung to recognise and subsequently formulate the concept of the collective unconscious and the archetypes.

Consistent with this pattern one can discover once again that it was from Jung's direct experience that he formulated the idea of the personal unconscious and the theory of complexes. It is, perhaps, this consistent derivation from actual personal or clinical experience that leads Jung to so consistently assert the fact that he is an empiricist, a person who deals with and discovers facts, rather than a theoretician. At first, such an assertion is seemingly absurd, when one takes a glance at the immense theoretical edifice that Jung created. However, I think that the facts speak for themselves, and that indeed Jung did derive and substantiate his theories from real life experience, whether it be personal or professional, if indeed there is, or ought to be, a distinction. It was while Jung was still occupied in his study of schizophrenic patients during his years as a psychiatrist in the Burghölzli Mental Asylum in Zürich that Jung turned his attention to another type of research, which has been termed the 'word-association experiment'. This well-known psychological test had originally been adapted from Wilhelm Wundt by Sir Francis Galton, a cousin of Charles Darwin's, to differentiate types of intelligence. In design it was extremely simple; the person being tested (the subject) was told that a series of words would be read out aloud, slowly, and that he or she was then to respond immediately to each word with the first word that came into her or his mind. Then, with a stop watch, the other person, the so-called examiner, noted the reaction time, that is, the seconds or fraction of seconds that it took a subject to reply by giving the first word that came into his or her mind. Usually, and this is true for Jung's early association experiments, there were about one hundred words. The actual test turned out to be of little value in actually measuring intelligence or types of intelligence, but Jung, from this failure, from noting that people varied in their response to certain words, from asking the basic question why does a highly intelligent person have difficulty in responding to a simple word that a child could answer, began the discovery of the whole field of complexes and the verification of a personal unconscious.

Wilhelm Wundt, the originator of the word-association test, had used it to explore conscious lines of thought. It occurred to Jung in about 1904 that he might be able to use this in his work. He was the first to use it to inquire into the disturbances in people's reactions, thus making it a valuable method for investigating the roots of mental illness. Difficulties that occurred in supplying a word in response to a given stimulus word alerted Jung to the entire notion of complexes. The fact that individuals varied enormously in their actual responses to particular words, in spite of, and indeed despite, their conscious intent, will and intelligence, alerted Jung to the existence of an unconscious realm in the psyche.

In short, what it proved was that delays in responding to words (that is, stimulus words) and faults in responding to them, such as mishearing the word or not hearing it at all, were not accidental lapses of memory or attention, but were determined with incredible precision by the disturbing effects that occurred in the unconscious mind in response to those particular words. That is, a specific word given as a stimulus had associations to other feelings, thoughts, memories, or whatever in the unconscious mind. Freud, of course, in a superb little book entitled *Psychopathology of Everyday Life,* had come to a similar conclusion as Jung, and had asserted that forgetting names of people we know, slips of tongue, are all indicators of unconscious conflict or associations in the area of the so-called mistake.

A simple example of this is from my own professional practice. A lady, in the course of the eighth interview with her, called me David instead of Peter. I noted this and asked about it, and she readily apologised for calling me the wrong name, but it alerted me to the possibility that there was some unconscious meaning associated with this slip of the tongue. I therefore asked her to associate for me what 'David' meant. Her association was that David was a young man who worked in her business, and in fact her description of David was 'he always lets me down on the big orders'. As it turned out, this woman's father had left her when she was eight, and this was the eighth interview, but at that time she had not discussed in any real detail the pain and disillusion of her father leaving her. In pointing out the meaning of the slip of the tongue to her, she replied that if I did not let her down then I would be the first person who hadn't. This simple example illustrates very adequately the relationship between slips of the tongue and powerful unconscious thoughts.

For Jung, these areas of conflict are called complexes, and in fact Jung's original title for his particular brand of psychology was 'complex psychology'. To recapitulate, what the word-association tests established beyond all reasonable doubt was that something within the individual of which he is more or less unaware – that is, something of which he is unconscious – could interfere with his conscious actions. Jung then set about to explore how these complexes came about, what were their nature and what constituted the realm of the personal unconscious.

In his Tavistock lectures delivered in London in 1935, Jung produced two or three very dramatic clinical examples of the word-association test and its capacity to unearth hidden complexes within the individual's psyche. The first subject was about forty-five years of age and so-called normal, but Jung observed that in his response to fifty stimulus words he had delayed responses – that is, much more delayed than his average response time – on five words. These words were knife, spear, to beat, pointed and bottle. Following disturbances of response ability on these five words, Jung turned to the man concerned and said, 'I did not know you had had such a disagreeable experience.' The man apparently mumbled something about not knowing what Jung was on about, and Jung continued: 'You know you were drunk and had a disagreeable affair with sticking your knife into somebody.' The man then reportedly confessed to an incident wherein he had got drunk and stabbed somebody, but because he had come from a very respectable family it had all been hushed up and he was left carrying the unresolved guilt feelings. So each word that was associated with this event, which had originally been the source of guilt, was unconsciously associated or connected, and therefore the reaction time – the time it took to respond to the words knife, spear, to beat, pointed and bottle – were delayed, and not the reaction time to the other forty-five words.

Personally, whilst I think this example very adequately demonstrates the law of association, I do not think it so adequately proves Jung's own point about complexes being unconscious, since to be unconscious the individual would have been unaware of the incident, unable to recall it, due to repression, whereas the fact that he confessed when confronted by Jung, attests to the fact that the specific event was well and truly in consciousness. However, another one of Jung's clinical examples, given in the same lectures at the Tavistock Clinic, does, I feel, both demonstrate the law of association – that is, how certain words are connected together through association with a particular feeling tone – *and* the relationship between these associated or linked ideas and an unconscious complex leading to conflict and mental disturbance.

I think that the feeling of Jung at work on such a complex and his use of the word-association test is perhaps best demonstrated and conveyed if I quote from his lecture. The case that Jung is discussing in this instance concerns a woman of approximately thirty years of age who was admitted to the clinic and given the diagnosis of schizophrenia of a depressive character.

I had this woman in my ward, and I had a peculiar feeling about her. I felt I could not agree with the bad prognosis, because already schizophrenia was a relative idea with me. I thought that we are all relatively crazy, but this woman was peculiar, and I could not accept the diagnosis as the last word. In those days one knew precious little. Of course I made an amnesis, but nothing was discovered that threw any light on her illness. Therefore I put her to the association test and finally made a very peculiar discovery. The first disturbance was caused by the word *angel,* and a complete lack of reaction by the word *obstinate.* Then there were *evil, blue, rich, stupid, dear,* and *to marry.* Now this woman was the wife of a well-to-do man in a very good position and apparently happy. I had questioned her husband and the only thing he could tell me, as she also did, was that the depression came on about two months after her eldest child had died – a little girl four years old. Nothing else could be found out about the aetiology of the case. The association test confronted me with a most baffling series of reactions which I could not put together. You will have been in such a situation, particularly if you have no routine with that kind of diagnosis. Then you first ask the test-person about the words which are not going directly to the kernel. If you asked directly about the strongest disturbances you would get wrong answers, so you begin with relatively harmless words and you are likely to get some honest replies. I said: 'What about angels? Does that word mean something to you?' She replied: 'Of course, that is my child whom I have lost.' And then came a great flood of tears. When the storm had blown over I asked: 'What does obstinate mean to you?' She said: 'It means nothing to me.' But I said: 'There was a big disturbance with the word and it means there is something connected with it.' I could not penetrate it. I came to the word evil and could get nothing out of her. There was a severely negative reaction which showed that she refused to answer. I went on to blue, and she said: 'Those are the eyes of the child I have lost.' I said: 'Did they make a particular impression on you?' She said: 'Of course, they were so wonderfully blue when the child was born.' I noticed the expression on her face, and I said: 'Why are you upset?' and she replied 'Well, she did not have the eyes of my husband.' Finally it came out that the child had had the eyes of a former lover of hers. I said: 'What is upsetting you with regard to that man?' and I was able to worm the story out of her.

In the little town in which she grew up there was a rich young man. She was of a well-to-do family but nothing grand. The man was of the moneyed aristocracy and the hero of the little town, and every girl dreamed of him. She was a pretty girl and thought she might have a chance. Then she discovered she had no chance with him, and her family said: 'Why think of him? He is a rich man and does not think of you. Here is Mr So-and-So, a nice man. Why not marry him?' She married him and was perfectly happy ever after until the fifth year of her marriage, when a former friend from her native town came to visit her. When her husband left the room he said to her: 'You have caused pain to a certain gentleman' (meaning the hero). She said: 'What? I caused pain?' The friend replied: 'Didn't you know he was in love with you and was disappointed when you married another man?' That set fire to the roof. But she repressed it. A fortnight later she was bathing her boy, two years, and her girl, four years. The water in the town – it was not in Switzerland – was not above suspicion, in fact it was infected with typhoid fever. She noticed that the little girl was sucking a sponge. But she did not interfere, and when the little boy said, 'I want to drink some water' she gave him the possibly infected water. The little girl got typhoid fever and died, the little boy was saved. Then she had what she wanted – or what the devil in her wanted – the denial of her marriage in order to marry the other man. To this end she had committed murder. She did not know it: she only told me the facts and did not draw the conclusion that she was responsible for the death of her child, since she knew the water was infected and there was danger. I was faced with the question of whether I should tell her she had committed murder, or whether I should keep quiet. (It was only a question of telling her, there was no threat of a criminal case.) I thought that if I told her it might make her condition much worse, but there was a bad prognosis anyhow, whereas, if she could realise what she had done, the chance was that she might get well. So I made up my mind to tell her point blank: 'You killed your child.' She went up in the air in an emotional state, but then she came down to the facts. In three weeks we were able to discharge her, and she never came back. I traced her for fifteen years and there was no relapse. That depression fitted her case psychologically: she was a murderess and under other circumstances would have deserved capital punishment. Instead of going to jail she was sent to the lunatic asylum. I practically saved her from the punishment of insanity by putting an enormous burden on her conscience. For if one can accept one's sins one can live with it. If one cannot accept it, one has to suffer the inevitable consequences.*

Apart from being a dramatic example of the way in which associations to words is highly systematic and informative and by no means accidental, this case also illustrates Jung's unrelenting conviction of the importance of finding the strength and courage simply to state what is and the relief that this simple statement can bring. So much of our energy is, I feel, tied up in maintaining complexes, keeping them out of consciousness, and yet often through simple slips of the tongue, inexplicable irrational outbursts, or the persistence of a seemingly odd and irrelevant idea in our head, we can gain access to the source of these complexes, thereby understand them, releasing the

**Analytical Psychology*, pp. 60-1. These lectures also appear in *CW* 18.

energy for perhaps more creative and constructive uses. For one of the basic truths of psychotherapy, reinforced time and time again, and made exquisitely clear by Jung, is that in making a complex conscious, the effect is one of reducing and often eliminating the effect of the complex on our everyday life. This is primarily because a complex, as Jung saw it, was like a split-off part of the psyche that had a tendency to behave like a partial, but separate, personality, often diametrically opposed to one's conscious wish and thereby often disturbing one's conscious behaviour.

Having said this much now, it seems to me appropriate that I provide some sort of definition of complex, a word that is so much in common usage these days that its precise meaning has been entirely vulgarised. Indeed the implication that lies behind the contemporary use of the word 'complex' is one of something 'imagined' by an individual, something that we have simply made up. Indeed, the further implication is that if the individual simply behaved 'sensibly' then the complex would not exist at all. Yet anyone who has a complex or complexes of any sort, for example an inferiority complex or a guilt complex, will know only too well that in spite of any deliberate and conscious attempts to behave oneself, or change one's ways, she or he will behave irrationally and repetitively in a contradictory direction to his or her conscious wishes. This is simply because the complex is based in the unconscious mind, is virtually an independent and separate personality, and until the source, the nucleus, is brought into consciousness no real change is possible. This is despite, and in fact in the face of, what I regard as the wishful thinking of so many psychologists these days who maintain, albeit ever so academically, the naïve view that self-talk will cure an individual of a complex. The point I could make is that it probably would cure the individual if the individual was consciously aware of what he was to talk himself or herself out of or into. But, in my view, no amount of endless listening to 'helpful' self-talk tapes, or advice-giving lectures, is ever going to resolve a complex. At best it may put a thin veneer on top of it, rendering it temporarily manageable until the necessary stimulus situation occurs again. However, in this day in which rationality and rational thinking is made a god, one can readily see how the hope or wishful thinking of many psychologists is that we can rationally talk ourselves out of a problem.

As Jung quite clearly said, we imagine we have a complex, when in fact the complex has us. This is because complexes and their sources have been repressed and are not available at the time to conscious thought; we can be alerted to their possible existence by, for example, slips of the tongue, forgetting, dreams, and other association phenomena as was so clearly elucidated in Jung's Tavistock lectures. According to Jung, complexes are:

> . . . psychic fragments which have split off owing to traumatic influences or certain incompatible tendencies. As the association experiments prove, complexes interfere with the intentions of the will and disturb the conscious performance, they produce disturbances of memory and blockages in the flow of association (the linking of ideas, perceptions, etc., according to similarities), they appear and disappear according

to their own laws; they can temporarily obsess consciousness, or influence speech and action in an unconscious way. In a word, complexes behave like independent beings. (*CW* 9:1:121)

It is in this sense that in spite of our conscious intent the complexes go on behaving and influencing our behaviour pretty well as they please, until they are brought into consciousness.

A few examples from my own professional experience may help to clarify even further the nature and origin of this realm of the personal unconscious that Jung has termed 'autonomous complexes'. In relation to these cases it is important to keep two further points in mind about the nucleus of a complex, and that is that it has two components, a dispositional and an environmental; that is, it is determined not only by experience, but also by the individual's way of reacting to that experience. Secondly, I personally hold the view that the eruption of a complex into consciousness is not accidental, but more often than not coincidental, the coincidence being derived from the function of association. The first example that I will give highlights this coincidence in which the timing of the eruption of the complex was in part determined by external events.

The woman concerned was in her early forties. The presenting problem was that her husband had left her and she found herself totally unable to manage her extremely strong depressive feelings, a tremendous fear that she was literally going to fall apart. This fear was not altogether invalid. However, given the woman's current situation and obvious indexes of professional confidence, the reaction of the fear appeared extremely excessive and well over and above what one would expect in such a situation. Her history revealed that her father had died unexpectedly of a heart attack when she was ten years of age, she being the only child. Her father was at the time of death forty-four years of age. The next four to six years of this woman's life were a complete and utter blank, except for the single memory of her mother standing motionless over the kitchen sink, crying. Her father's death was never ever spoken of! She recalled that about at fourteen years of age (just after coming into puberty), while visiting a girlfriend feeling very envious when she observed the girl sitting on her father's knee. She remembered reacting to this extremely strongly by having a powerful urge to visit her father's grave, and indeed, somewhat tragically, on the one occasion she tried to do so she found the gates locked and remembered standing there, shaking the gates and crying. There were no further memories of her father. She subsequently got married, following a traditional courtship, preceded by a period of tremendous awkwardness and shyness with boys. The marriage seemingly went well until two years before I saw her, and at that time her own daughter was ten years of age, the exact age she had been when her father died. The next two years were reported by her as extremely difficult, with no communication, 'just a deadness'. These two years finally culminated in her husband leaving her, just as he himself was rising forty-four! The two events, beginning with the daughter turning ten years of age and culminating in her husband approaching forty-four reawakened in this woman the underlying father complex. This complex manifested itself in her by her perception of men being almost dominated by a sense of grief, loss, and a feeling of abandonment, which was associated with her father dying. Indeed, I would go so far as to say that this father complex acted autonomously in her unconscious, just as Jung indicates, virtually determining the nature of her relationship to men to the extent that unconsciously she expected her husband to die at forty-four, and indeed she probably unconsciously brought about the separation by this expectation. He partially confirmed this by telling me that he did not know why he left, he just 'felt he had to go', that his wife 'was pushing him out', telling him he should leave. To my mind this provides a clear example of Jung's definition of a complex, and clearly indicates the powerful and autonomous effect it can have on an individual's life.

The second example concerns a guilt complex. Briefly this focuses on a woman of thirty-five years of age whose history again involved a father leaving, only this time through separation rather than death, when the girl was twelve years of age. She reacted by becoming sexually promiscuous, resulting in her becoming pregnant and having an abortion at thirteen years of age. Bear in mind, then, that an abortion in Melbourne, Australia, twenty years ago was a most distasteful and seedy experience, sure to evoke powerful feelings of guilt, remorse and shame. At thirty-five years of age she found herself in her second marriage, unhappily so, and unexpectedly conceived to her husband, since in recent times there had been no sexual life at all between them. She was very ambivalent about staying in the marriage and decided to have the foetus aborted. This resulted in a massive period of internal chaos, again the feeling of terror of actually coming apart, accompanied by intense remorse and grief. Despite the fact that the decision had been made rationally in the cold light of day, what of course had happened was that this abortion had reawakened all the guilt and associated feelings from the first abortion, which had been repressed and never dealt with. The guilt complex had also been associated with her perception of herself as a mother, and indeed she constantly felt she was merely role-playing as a mother. In her own words, 'I could not connect to being a mother.' Working through of the guilt complex reawakened by the second abortion had the effect, not unexpectedly so, of reconnecting her to the sense of being a mother again. One can see here the autonomous nature of complexes and their role in determining everyday conscious behaviour. This woman had never ever grieved or dealt with her first abortion, it was her unexpected pregnancy and the second abortion that had reawakened the autonomous guilt complex that was lurking in her unconscious mind and which had interfered with her capacity to form a relationship with her own children. Some complexes are obviously more serious than others. But either way they are for ever lurking in the shadows, constantly seeking expression and thereby disrupting our normal conscious behaviour.

SHADOW FIGURES

The use of the word 'shadow' provides a very neat link to the next structure within the personal unconscious and that is the shadow. Jung defined this aspect of the personal unconscious as follows:

> The shadow personifies every thing that the subject refuses to acknowledge about himself and yet is always thrusting itself upon him, directly or indirectly – for instance inferior traits of character and other incompatible tendencies. (*CW* 9:1:284)

In other words, the shadow is the inferior part of the personality, the sum of all personal and collective psychic elements which, because of their incompatibility with the chosen conscious attitude, are denied expression in conscious life and therefore coalesce into a relatively autonomous splinter personality with contrary tendencies in the unconscious mind. This shadow systematically behaves in a compensatory (that is, balancing) manner in relation to consciously held attitudes, views, etc. Hence its effect on our everyday conscious life can be both positive as well as negative.

In short, whatever aspects of your ego-conscious self is unacceptable will tend to be personified in the unconscious mind as a shadow figure of which we can have many. Hence it differs from a complex only in so far as it is not a specific trauma that pushes it into the unconscious, but rather what we ourselves, aided and abetted by the family and other significant adults whom we grow up with, push into unconsciousness. It normally appears in dreams as a personality of the same sex whereas the anima, or animus, usually appears in our dreams as a member of the opposite sex. The shadow can also manifest itself, and indeed often does, in the outside world by the mechanism of projection.

That is, we put onto someone else, usually of the same sex, the unconscious and thereby unacceptable shadow traits of ourselves. Hence repetitive conflict with someone of the same sex, our *bête noire,* as the French would call it, is usually indicative of shadow motivated behaviour. It is always 'the other person's fault' that tells us that our shadow is speaking. However, I should quickly point out that the shadow is not necessarily negative. It can in some instances be composed of entirely positive aspects, since the shadow (the dark side of consciousness) is simply a personification or a series of personifications of what is unacceptable to our conscious view of ourselves.

It is simplistic in the extreme to assume that it is simply bad. In fact, some personalities in which consciousness is characterised by a negative attitude, where spontaneity and generosity and other positive traits have been repressed because they were unacceptable in the family, in such an individual this shadow may well be a positive figure. The following dream I think highlights the positive aspect of the shadow. The girl concerned was in her late twenties, her mother had been a chronic depressive personality throughout the girl's life and particularly during adolescence, thereby good feelings, positive feelings, had been associated in this girl's mind with causing her mother's depressive reaction and thereby taking on a negative connotation. Indeed, within this family positive feelings were totally unacceptable, for to further complicate matters, her father was a policeman who found fun and play unacceptable to himself. So on both fronts the girl's personality was determined by a rejection of positive aspects. Here, then, is the dream:

I remember visiting an old flatmate of mine who is now married and living in the country. We were in Melbourne at a flat having dinner with her parents. I don't remember having much contact with them on the night, rather I talked with Lynn for most of the time. She used to be untidy and keen to put down the aesthetic side of life. Today though she had a beautiful bright pink dinner setting which sat up on legs and had a Japanese blue-and-white design on it. We talked about this dinner set, I held it and felt very warm with the experience. I accidentally knocked this fragile set and though I wasn't sure, and Lynn said it wasn't me, I think I chipped a plate. We began talking about what we were each doing. Lynn said she and her mother had been shopping and had bought three or four nice pieces of clothing. Again I thought this was a change as Lynn was never a spender. She showed me the clothes, bright pink and aqua blue. I really loved the colours and was eager to go shopping myself. I went down to the local shopping centre and I walked around, saw nothing, and ended up in an exclusive restaurant, which had paintings of Napoleon Bonaparte around. There was a brightly coloured statue of Napoleon laid out [that is, dead]. I walked through the restaurant and into the descending lift under the clock tower. There were about six people in the run-down lift with marble flooring. When we reached the ground floor I found that the only way was back the way I had originally walked around; past many hairdressing salons, a tempting coffee shop, up the stairs and into the dress shops again. I was tired of walking around by this time and thought back to my meal with Lynn; she had found what she was looking for, why couldn't I?

In contrast to this girl's everyday life the same-sex figure in the dreams (Lynn) is a very happy, bright girl (as indicated by the bright colours) and has seemingly a good relationship with her mother. In this sense it could be seen as the opposite or repressed part of the girl herself and the dream incidentally indicates that the way in which to get back, to get in touch with this positive shadow part of herself is to descend in the old lift, that is to go back into the unconscious, and come back the same way as she has been before; that is past the dress shops, which can be seen as a means of taking on a new attitude. It is not uncommon for the shadow figure to appear as an old school friend in dreams since, in my view, very often it is in the beginning of adolescence that we are forced to repress one side of our personality in the interest of the other. The shadow figure can also appear in dreams as a sibling and the following dream indicates this very well.

I was with my sister Cynthia, getting ready for work I think, hurrying quite a deal and she was talking a lot. I was looking for my shower cap and when I found it there was rubbish inside it (Kleenex, empty talcum bottles, powder dust) and I emptied it, puzzled and annoyed. But I was loath to place it on my head afterwards; then I saw my current shower cap on the floor and it was very wet. The implication in the dream was that Cynthia had just used it and I was a bit annoyed with her because she hadn't put it back in its customary place.

The dreamer in this case was a thirty-year-old single girl who could be best characterised by having

U.J.—4

an over-developed intellectual side of her personality and a repression of her feelings, her warmth and spontaneity. When I discussed the dream with her, her association to her sister was that she was a very lively, extroverted, warm and outgoing personality. Thus the sister can be seen as the positive warm and shadow aspect of the dreamer herself, and in the dream one can make the interpretation that the shower cap represents something that you put on your head – that is, an intellectualised attitude – and the dreamer was annoyed that Cynthia, the warm, extroverted, outgoing part of herself, had in fact not put it back in its customary place. That is, her feeling side, her warm and outgoing side, had temporarily disturbed her intellectualised side. The preceding two dreams tend to focus on the positive shadow aspect; the next dream indicates a more traditional shadow, that is the negative side of a personality. The dreamer was in fact the same person that I referred to in the section of complexes who had lost her father at the age of ten and whose husband had subsequently separated from her. This is the dream:

I was turning left into Gully Road on my way to visit my husband's flat. Suddenly, as I turned the corner, the car got out of control. It spun around and around and around and finally spinning up and landing in the forest. I then found myself walking up the street with a dark shadowy woman, theatrical, moustache drawn on her face, and dressed like Big Bird from Sesame Street, only instead of being in yellow she was dressed in all black. She kept talk, talk, talk all the time and I found her a very dominating bore. There was an awful evil feeling about her.

This dream clearly indicates the negative shadow side of this woman that threatened to be destructive throughout her entire life, and indeed one that had a very negative effect on her life.

A final example in connection with the shadow comes from a man's dream, which highlights the fact that the shadow can sometimes be personified in dreams as being opposite us; that is, being in the opposite position to consciousness. This following dream also highlights the role of a figure that we have yet to discuss, and that is the anima figure in a man, or the feminine side of his personality. The dreamer was a thirty-four-year-old man who had been divorced for eighteen months and previously been married for eight years. He was a very quiet, introverted man, who had considerable difficulty in expressing his feelings and occasionally found himself overwhelmed by a very rich fantasy life that threatened to disrupt his ordinary conscious behaviour. Here, then, is the dream:

I am travelling on a train, the driver is an overweight girl who I consider asking for a date because I am lonely, but, however, do not because she is fat and ugly. There are secret compartments on the train which I may use when I wish to escape from undesirable people who won't leave me alone. I overhear a rough young woman sharing her problems with another and looking across at me, considering whether to put the bite on me for some money. This happens and although I expect these approaches (hence the secret passages) this girl seems manageable and I'd like to help. She asked if I'd make a loan and produces her bona fides at the suggestion of her friend – a large document to show that her husband has failed to pay maintenance. There is an envelope stapled to the inside which, however, the friend rips out so that I won't examine it. I know that I am being taken for a ride. I apologise and say that I have no money. In fact, I have a wallet full of money! The loan is only for a night on the town anyway and I'm not inclined to join in despite the inferred offer, should I supply the money. Another passenger who has been listening in, a man passenger, suggests that they rob a 'phone box for some money. This man was sitting opposite me in the train and I advised against turning to crime, even petty crime, when the solution in this case was to beat the hell out of the erstwhile husband and obtain the maintenance money. We seemed to depart on reasonable terms, though I find myself checking my wallet and checking that it hasn't been lifted or any money removed.

This is a very complex dream in many ways and depicts the man's unconscious attitude towards the feminine part of himself; that is, he sees it as some part that is threatening to exploit and use him. The relevant figure within the present context of shadows is the man who sits opposite the dreamer and suggests that he robs the telephone box in order to acquire money to meet the female passenger's needs. We find that this figure is in juxtaposition to the dreamer, who finds himself in the dream suggesting that the solution is to 'beat the hell out of the erstwhile husband'. These two male figures in the dream I believe depict the two shadows within this man, one that resorts to devious and secretive means for meeting his needs and the other who meets his needs through aggression. In many respects this conflict within the unconscious reflects this man's problems in finding a workable balance between being totally withdrawn and devious or, on the other hand, being outgoing and aggressive.

In addition to the manifestations of the shadow figure in dreams and in repetitive conflicts with members of our own sex in the outside world, another fascinating place that shadow figures turn up is in fairytales and literature; for example, in the classic Robert Louis Stevenson novel *Dr Jekyll and Mr Hyde*. That shadow figures show up in creative literary works ought not be too surprising, since true creative work springs from the unconscious mind; very often it simply represents the writer's, or painter's or musician's unconscious content. With respect to fairytales, what is generally not well known is that until the seventeenth century fairytales were not reserved for children, but were told among grown-ups, that is adult people, amongst woodcutters and peasants, etc., for amusement. In addition, one can see in fairytales the remnants of the myth-making activity that we have spoken of before, and therefore they are very often reflective of unconscious material, presented in story form, passed on from one generation to another. The fact that we, in modern times, have relegated fairytales to the realm and province of children is simply reflective of our collective rejection of the irrational aspects of ourselves and that pronounced tendency to regard the unconscious and its manifestations as infantile or belonging to children. Hence the collective shadow in some ways of Western civilisation, of our technological civilisation, is, I suspect, characterised by irrationality, since this represents the repressed aspect of consciousness. The following Grimm Brothers fairytale is a fine example of the unconscious wisdom and knowledge contained in fairy stories. This one is called the 'Two Travellers' and it is highly symbolic, I believe, of the problems of the shadow figure.

Mountain and valley do not meet, but human beings sometimes do, both good and bad. So it happened that a tailor and a shoemaker met in the wandering. The tailor was a small, good looking, amusing and merry sort of fellow. He saw the shoemaker on the other side of the road and greeted him with a joke. But the shoemaker did not like jokes and made a sour face and looked like biting the tailor, but the little fellow began to laugh and handed him his bottle saying, 'No harm meant – have a drink and swallow your rage.' The shoemaker took a big draught and suggested that they should walk on together. 'All right,' said the tailor, 'if you want to go to a big town where there is plenty of work.'

The tailor, always merry and fresh and red-cheeked, had no trouble in getting work, as well as a kiss behind the door from the master's daughter, and when he met the shoemaker always had more money than he. Although the surly shoemaker was not so fortunate, the tailor laughed and shared what he had with his companion. When they had been some time on the road, they came to a big forest through which a way led to the King's city. But there were two paths; one took seven days and the other only two, and they didn't know which was which and debated as to the quantity of bread they should take. The shoemaker wanted to take enough for seven days, but the tailor was ready to take a risk and trust in God. It was a long way. By the third day the tailor had finished his bread, but the shoemaker had no pity on him. By the fifth day the tailor was so hungry that he asked the shoemaker for some bread, for he was quite white and exhausted. The shoemaker agreed, but said that in exchange the tailor must let him put out one of his eyes. The unhappy tailor, who didn't want to die, could only agree, and the heartless shoemaker cut out his right eye. The next day the tailor was again hungry and on the seventh day too exhausted to stand. The shoemaker then said that he would have pity on him and give him more bread, but that in return he must have the tailor's other eye.

Then the tailor begged forgiveness for the light-hearted way in which he had lived and told the shoemaker that he had not deserved such treatment at his hands, for he had always shared everything with him and without his eyes he would not be able to sew and could only beg, and he asked that he might not be left there to die alone in his blindness. But the shoemaker, who had shut God out of his heart, took his knife and cut out the left eye. Then he gave the tailor a piece of bread, cut him a stick and led him away. When the sun went down they came out of the woods by some gallows. There the shoemaker led the blind tailor and left him. Worn out with pain and hunger the tailor fell asleep and slept through the whole night. When he woke in the morning he did not know where he was. On the gallows hung two poor sinners and on the head of each sat a crow. The two crows began to talk and one told the other that the dew which during the night had fallen on them from the gallows would give back sight to anyone who washed with it. When the tailor heard that he took his handkerchief and soaked it in the dew on the grass, washed his eye sockets with it, and his two healthy eyes.*

This particular story goes on quite considerably, with many more adventures for the tailor and the shoemaker, finally resulting in the tailor being triumphant over the shoemaker. However, the important point to know for our present context is that the fairytale quite deliberately from the outset deals with both good and bad, that is with shadow aspects. The tailor on the one hand can be seen as a fairly extroverted personality with an easygoing, happy-go-lucky nature who says 'no harm meant – have a drink and swallow your rage'. In other words, the tailor can be seen as a fairly superficial person, whereas the shoemaker, on the other hand, can be seen as taciturn, depressing and an aggressive person. The story then as it unfolds shows the interaction between these two characters with finally the conscious attitude represented by the tailor being virtually destroyed by the unconscious or shadow aspect represented by the shoemaker. The final part of the story shows the resolution, or at least the resolution for this part of the fairytale, in the tailor being left under the gallows and informed by the crows that if he washes his eyes with dew he will have his sight restored. In symbolic terms, terms which we will deal with in later chapters,

**Tales of Grimm and Anderson,* with an Introduction by W. H. Auden, Random House Modern Library Series, 1952, pp. 285-92.

the crow can be seen as symbolic of intuition and the dew as symbolic of feeling. In other words, the fairy-tale indicates that by restoring his intuitive level and by developing his feelings the tailor in fact had his sight restored, that is can see once again where he is heading.

One can also find adequate reference to the shadow and shadow figures in poetry. For example, T. S. Eliot in 'The Hollow Men' has the following lines:

> Between the idea
> And the reality
> Between the motion
> And the act
> Falls the shadow.
>
> Between the conception
> And the creation
> Between the emotion
> And the response
> Falls the shadow.
>
> Between the desire
> And the spasm
> Between the potency
> And the existence
> Between the essence
> And the descent
> Falls the shadow.

How to deal with one's shadow is a psychological problem to which there is no short answer and no short cuts other than to say it is a life's work. A start can most certainly be made by recognising what have been termed 'projections', by coming to grips with the fact that the person one detests so fervently – or indeed, on the other hand, the person one admires so fervently, that is, idealises – is more often than not one's shadow side. But facing the shadow side and withdrawing projections is, by and large, not a happy or easy experience. Nevertheless it is the first task that needs to be accomplished if psychological growth is to occur. Pouring nice warm feelings mixed up with excessive doses of empathy and unconditional positive regard is all very nice (peculiarly American, like toasted marshmallow and popcorn), however it will not facilitate confrontation with one's shadow or shadows. Confronting it in some people brings on feelings of insufferable guilt, powerful feelings of having wasted one's life, of having lived a life of self-deception. So in some it creates a feeling of hopelessness, in others a feeling of panic, and in yet others a feeling of impossibility.

It is little wonder, then, that most people leave their shadows where they are; that is, firmly planted, nailed down, and fixed on someone else. This 'fixing on someone else' explains so much of repetitive conflictual relationships between people of the same sex that otherwise seems to defy rational explanation. Indeed the task of integrating or recognising the shadow is at times so difficult that it is reasonably well established that analysis or psychotherapy can break down, rapidly terminate, once the shadow appears. This rapid or premature termination can take the form, on one hand, of the person receiving psychotherapy suddenly deciding, albeit prematurely, that they are well and no longer need psychotherapy; this phenomena called a flight into health. On the other hand, the more depressive and pessimistic personality is simply likely to declare that the psychotherapy is useless and that change is impossible. Whether the premature termination is the optimistic one or the pessimistic one is really irrelevant; what both solutions in the form of premature termination represent is the very real and painful difficulty of coming to grips with one's shadow side.

Jung himself recognised only too well the difficulties in coming to grips with the shadow side of our personalities and accepting them and integrating them into ego-consciousness. He had this to say about the process.

If you imagine someone who is brave enough to withdraw all these projections, then you get an individual who is conscious of a considerable shadow. Such a man has saddled himself with new problems and complexes. He has become a serious problem to himself as he is now unable to say *they* do this or that, *they* are wrong, and *they* must be fought against. Such a man knows that whatever is wrong in the world is wrong in himself.*

Jung's words 'brave enough' capture the very real difficulty of this task. However, as the shadow is a substantial and very real part of ourselves, it is here that true psychological work commences, in the recognition and withdrawing of projections and finally the acceptance of the dark and unconscious side of our own personalities.

**Psychology and Religion,* volume 11 of *CW,* p. 83.

PERSONA

The final structure of personal unconscious that we need to discuss is the persona. Originally persona referred to the masks that actors in antiquity used. Within the Jungian framework the persona is the mask or façade (in proper social circles, the role!) that one exhibits publicly. It might also be adequately called the conformity archetype. Jung called the persona the outward face of the psyche because it is the face that the world sees. It is therefore a necessity, and through it, acted out in roles, we relate to the outside world. It has the effect of simplifying our contacts with each other, and clarifies what we might expect from them, thereby taking some of the anxiety out of everyday living and social exchange.

However, there is ever present within the persona the danger of identifying oneself with the mask; or another way of saying that is identifying one's true self with the role that one fills. If this happens, the person thereby loses contact with the deeper sources of their own being and indeed life itself becomes one ongoing role-play behind which the person, the Self, disappears, and this results in a denial of the rest of the personality. One can sense this when it has happened, since there exists a peculiar state of deadness in people who have shrivelled back and hidden behind their masks, a sort of psychological mummification. Sometimes we might find ourselves saying things like 'he just plays a part'. You are then left wondering who it is that they really are behind their part. Thus while a mask (or indeed several masks) is a necessary and vital piece of social equipment useful for social lubrication, the task of being, as we shall come to discuss explicitly in the chapter on individuation, is to strive to complete ourselves; that is, to bring into the light of consciousness *all* of who we are. To hide behind a mask, in the words of Soren Kierkegaard, is to condemn oneself to a life of 'half obscurity'.

4. Psychological Types

In each of the previous chapters I have endeavoured to articulate Jung's contribution to our understanding of mind and also attempted to demonstrate how, with courage and insight, he drew on his own personal and professional life. Jung is, in my opinion, an example *par excellence* of a man who took the task of being conscious of oneself seriously and indeed there is unequivocal evidence that his life was an ongoing struggle for consciousness.

It is no accident, albeit not entirely conscious planning on my part, that the first three chapters took as their primary focus the unconscious mind, since this is entirely consistent with Jung's view that consciousness emerges out of the unconscious. Thus the present chapter focuses on Jung's major and lasting contribution to the psychology of consciousness, which is largely embodied or contained in his work entitled *Psychological Types,* which constitutes volume 6 of his *Collected Works.*

The content of the first three chapters has also paralleled stages in Jung's personal life. The first, focusing on his family background and childhood, laid the groundwork for developing an appreciation of what myth-making moved Jung, what experiences and phenomena he was endeavouring to make sense of. The second chapter focused on his early professional career as a psychiatrist, drawing particularly on his clinical experience of, and confrontation with, schizophrenic patients, leading to his articulation of the concept of the collective unconscious and the archetypes. The third chapter paralleled this period also, although a slightly later stage of it, when, through the use of the word-association test, Jung developed the theory of autonomous complexes. The content of this chapter again parallels Jung's personal life and refers to that period building up to and culminating in his break from Sigmund Freud.

It was through his publication of *The Psychology of Dementia Praecox* in 1906 that Jung came to know Freud and began an association that lasted until 1913, approximately seven years. Despite an early and enthusiastic sharing of ideas between Jung and Freud, remembering that their first meeting in Vienna in 1907 lasted for, in Jung's words, 'thirteen uninterrupted hours', it was not long before differences in outlook emerged, primarily around their respective views of symbols and the symbolic process and the place of sexuality; specifically the Oedipus complex in the theory of the psyche and its development.

These differences came to a head in 1912 at the Fourth Psychoanalytical Congress, held in Munich. It was at this Congress that Freud's infamous fainting spell in response to an argument over the father complex with Jung took place. It was also at this Congress that Jung's *Psychology of the Unconscious* (renamed *Symbols of Transformation*) came under fire, and Freud was unable to accept Jung's view as a legitimate development of psychoanalysis. It was at this Congress that the parting of the ways took place and Jung withdrew from the Freudian School. However, as a reading of *Memories, Dreams and Reflections* shows, Jung was considerably distressed by the emotional controversy, yet despite his personal involvement he was the only person to realise that a difference of opinion of such dimensions must not be seen simply as a personal disagreement on a specific issue. To Jung, the fact that two obviously highly intelligent and unquestionably sincere investigators were unable to agree on a matter of major importance was in itself a psychological problem. For Jung to reduce it in the way that most people do, down to an absurdly simplistic conclusion that he was right and Freud was wrong or vice versa, would not have been feasible or sensible. Jung believed that the dispute with Freud rested on essential differences in their assumptions about the mind, in particular the unconscious mind. Jung, reflecting his not inconsiderable wisdom and capacity to live a conscious life, felt he could hardly be impartial in discussing and assessing his differences with Freud, and yet he records that he wanted to approach and work out the psychological problem. This appears to have been contradictory to Freud's view, which is recorded in a biography of Freud written by Ernest Jones. Freud announced the breaking off of his personal relationship with Jung thus:

> I consider there is no hope of rectifying the errors of the Zürich people and believe that in two or three years we shall be moving in two entirely different directions with no mutual understanding . . . the best way to guard against any bitterness is an attitude of expecting nothing at all, [i.e. the worst].*

*Ernest Jones, *The Life and Work of Sigmund Freud* (abridged edition), Hogarth Press, 1962, p. 324.

The fact that they were going in different directions in two or three years is undoubtedly correct, however the guarding against bitterness seems short lived or inadequately defended against, since in a letter written to Ernest Jones shortly after the final split with Jung, Freud had this to say:

It may be that we overrate Jung and his doings in the next time. He is not in a favourable position before the public when he turns against me [i.e. his past]. But my general judgement on the matter is very much like yours. I expect no immediate success but incessant struggling. Anyone who promises to mankind liberation from the hardship of sex will be hailed as a hero, let him talk whatever nonsense he chooses.*

Jung, nevertheless, unlike Freud, was not simply satisfied in accepting the inevitable differences in directions, but as already mentioned was determined to seek some understanding of them. While in Vienna he had met Dr Alfred Adler, who had been one of Freud's earliest followers and who subsequently had had many heated disagreements with Freud and was the first notable to defect from Freud. Jung decided that by studying the psychology of the split between Freud and Adler he might throw some light on his own dispute and split with Freud.

In essence what emerged was that he undertook a comparative study of an actual case of neurosis and applied both Freud's and Adler's theories to the case. He concluded that each theory had adequately explained the psychopathology of the case and decided

*Ibid. p. 326.

that a neurosis can be understood in opposing or contradictory ways. Since for Adler a neurosis had a purpose, an objective, primarily to protect the patient from failure, to put responsibility away from oneself. According to Adler he held that, above all else, individuals were motivated to seek security and supremacy, and whether an individual was, or was not, inferior, he felt it, and his goal therefore was to achieve a sense of power within himself. Hence, in the simplest possible terms, neurosis in Adler's view was a mechanism for avoiding failure by creating devices, symptoms, for never entering the rat-race in the first place. By contrast, Freud's view of neurosis at the time was that neuroses were directly caused by the manner in which a child coped with the Oedipus complex.

Jung's conclusion about these seemingly incompatible theories, and yet adequate opposing explanations was, in his own words:

> Each investigator most readily sees that factor in the neurosis which corresponds to his peculiarity . . . each sees things from a different angle and thus they evolve fundamentally different views and theories. This difference can hardly be anything else but a difference of temperament, a contrast between two different types of human mentality, one of which finds the determining agent pre-eminently in the subject [Adler] and the other in the object [Freud] . . . I have finally, on the basis of numerous observations and experiences, come to postulate two fundamental attitudes, namely, introversion and extroversion.

* *Two Essays on Analytical Psychology,* volume 7 of *CW,* pp. 40-3.

In the simplest possible terms, Jung concluded that Freud and Adler were basically different types, Freud an extrovert and Adler an introvert. It was Jung then who introduced these terms to twentieth-century psychology; terms that have now become part of our everyday language. In extroversion the prevalent flow of psychic energy is outward, the conscious contents of the psyche refer, in the main, to external objects or events. In introversion, the conscious contents refer more to the individual's subjective or inner world and the flow of psychic energy is inwards towards the inner world. For the extrovert external events are all-important and influence his life. By contrast, for the introvert, what constitutes events for him is their subjective meaning and his subjective response is of prime concern. In essence, therefore, introversion and extroversion are opposing directions of psychic energy flow and represent two fundamentally different attitudes towards life. There is, of course, no 'pure type' since, as Jung states:

Every individual possesses both mechanisms – extroversion as well as introversion, and only the relative predominance of the one over the other determines the type.*

Although each individual does possess both types, it is very characteristic of each type to denigrate the other, seeing the negative rather than the positive qualities of the opposite type. This is because we tend to develop one attitude over and above the other, placing one firmly in consciousness and the other equally

**Psychological Types*, volume 6 of *CW*, p. 4.

firmly in the unconscious, whereby it becomes a shadow figure. Hence the denigration of the opposite type to our conscious type is simply a projection of this rejected aspect of our selves, the shadow aspects, onto a suitably deemed outsider.

I think it reasonably accurate to say that in the Western World we value extroverts, describing them in such favourable terms as outgoing, sociable, well-adjusted, etc., while the introvert in the West is often dubbed self-centred, withdrawn, anti-social, and even morbid. By contrast, in the East, by and large it is the introverted attitude that is valued and the extroverted that is devalued. It seems as if there may well exist a biological basis for introversion and extroversion, and Jung does not dispute this, nor does he particularly affirm it. However, what is clear is that in any one family one can find introverts and extroverts with the former usually being overshadowed by their more sociable, extroverted brother or sister.

The earliest signs of an extroverted child is usually his or her quick adaptation to the outside world, his environment. He or she usually approaches objects unhesitatingly, with little caution and usually little fear; it is an active and confident reaching out into the environment. In short, everything unknown seems alluring. Such a child is usually the sort that teachers, reflecting the prevalent bias in our Western society, describe as being 'well-adjusted with satisfactory social relationships'!

The introverted child, by comparison, is shy and hesitant. He or she usually dislikes new situations, and usually approaches new objects or events with caution, some fear, and on many occasions suspicion. The introverted child usually prefers to play alone and have one, rather than many, friends. Such children are often thoughtful and have a very rich imaginative world. However, equally often are they the cause of anxiety to their parents, who equate introversion with maladjustment, again reflecting the prevalent Western bias. At the adult level, all one simply sees in terms of extroversion and introversion is a development of these basic trends that have already been observable in childhood.

EXTROVERTED ADULT

The extroverted adult is sociable, he meets others halfway – sometimes more than halfway – and is often interested in anything and everything. Many extroverts like listening to the radio or watching television as a background noise while they are doing something else; they need to have outside input. They usually like organisations, groups, community gatherings and parties; in short they are active and the sort of person who is usually described as a good person for getting things going. They have a good relationship with the outside world and tend to be both optimistic and enthusiastic, though often their enthusiasm is short lived, as also can be their relationships with other people. In fact, the weakness or shadow side, if you like, of extroverts lies in their tendency to be superficial and their dependence on making a good impression – classically the good salesperson. Extroverts as a rule enjoy nothing more than an audience and tend to dislike being alone, regarding introspection or reflection as morbid or unhealthy. In fact, extroverts will usually circumvent any move, either from within themselves or others, to introspect or reflect on their inner world and meaning.

The extrovert sometimes circumvents sorting out his own feelings and ideas by belonging to an organised set of ideas, such as a church. In his adjustment the extrovert orientates himself predominantly by the social norms, the spirit of the times – he is a consensus man and absolutely vital for any communal life or society.

INTROVERTED ADULTS

Introverted adults, on the other hand, dislike society and feel lonely and lost in large gatherings. They tend to be sensitive, often unduly so, and afraid of making a fool of themselves and appearing ridiculous. They sometimes seem unable to learn how to behave in social situations, appearing clumsy, at times behaving inappropriately, and at other times they are rather ridiculously polite, almost obsequious. They also tend to be over-conscientious, primarily because they are uncertain, and cautious regarding the outside world, pessimistic and critical. In organisations, or for that matter society, they tend to be overlooked because, unlike their extroverted colleagues, they can display their abilities only in sympathetic surroundings, whereas the extrovert only needs an audience, sometimes only an audience of one, to evoke a full-blooded display of his or her self-perceived gifts or talents.

Interestingly enough, introverted adults often seem to me to possess unusual knowledge, perhaps because they are at their best when alone and quiet in such pursuits as reading. Unlike extroverts, introverts do not tend to be people of their 'times', they can quite often display a marked resistance to 'going along with the trend', and tend to display an independence of judgement, sometimes ignoring quite important external facts. The major weakness of an introverted personality lies in their danger of becoming under-involved due to their insistence on preserving their separateness. In becoming under-involved the risk is of losing contact with the outside world altogether, and then the appearance of aloofness and snobbishness, which introverts can give, becomes readily apparent.

Whilst Jung maintained that his typology of extrovert and introvert was a classification of the normal, either type can of course become neurotic or even psychotic. The previous comment regarding the major weaknesses of the introverted personality introduces this topic, and it is probably important to pay some brief attention to this before moving on to the four functions.

In mental disturbances the extrovert tends to go to the extreme end of the extroverted continuum and lose touch altogether with his or her inner or introverted world. Whereas for the introvert, as I have already indicated, disturbances for him or her manifest themselves in a loss of contact with external or outer reality. Jung's own view was that extroverts, when they became neurotic, display hysterical symptoms in which anxiety and its various manifestations are the major ingredients, and in which the symptoms are often highly symbolic and not uncommonly related to sexual issues or conflicts. In more serious psychotic disturbances, a neo-psychoanalytic view is that extroverts tend to become manic-depressives, showing marked swings between being extremely and inappropriately active and happy, with a deluded sense of well-being and, on the other hand, being utterly immobilised by depression. In short, the traditional analytic view is that mania (heightened activity characteristic of extroverts) is a defence mechanism against underlying feelings of depression; that is, the activity is in direct proportion to the intensity of the depressive feeling being avoided. In Jungian terms, one can see that the absolute withdrawal characteristic of depression is reflective of the unconscious or compensatory introversion of the conscious extroverted attitude.

When introverts become disturbed, they tend to become obsessional and preoccupied with ordering their world; that is, rendering it more reliable, predictable and less frightening. In the psychotic disturbances of introverts, as one would expect, given their natural movement towards uninvolvement with external reality, they tend to become more emotionally isolated and suffer a loss of meaning so characteristic of the extreme forms of schizophrenia. That is, they demonstrate a complete break with the outside world. It does seem that illness in introverts is more serious than extroverts, since the evidence or view appears to be that 'manic-depressives recover, at any rate from any given attack, whereas schizophrenics show a strong tendency to become inmates of mental institutions'.*

For those who are familiar with the work of Melanie Klein, I think one could say that the extrovert, when he or she becomes disturbed, regresses to the depressive position, whereas the introvert, when he or she

*Storr, *Jung*, p. 73.

becomes ill, regresses farther back to the early point of emotional fixation, the paranoid-schizoid position in which only a very sketchy or patchy awareness of objects in the external world exists. Hence in this position relationships are only with the internal object, which makes therapy extremely difficult, if not impossible. What mental illness, whether it be neurosis or psychosis, represents with respect to introversion and extroversion, and, indeed, as we shall see shortly with respect to the four functions, is that one aspect has been over-developed or over-emphasised, causing the other to be severely repressed into the unconscious mind. Jung himself attempted to put introversion and extroversion on an equal footing, on the basis that man needed to relate both to his inner world thus to 'introvert' his libido or psychic energy *and* also to connect to his outer world, to 'extrovert' his libido. The over-development of one aspect results in an imbalance of the psyche, which causes neurosis or a psychosis. Between extroversion and introversion there exists a compensatory relationship; that is, where consciousness is extroverted, the unconscious is introverted. So when the opposite side comes through, as it can by a projection, it tends to be primitive and under-developed, so that, for example, a positive-minded extroverted man living at peace with his outside world can become temporarily or permanently a critical, distrustful person who suspects everyone's motives. Such a change, as we will discuss later, can be a sure sign that the psychological crises associated with mid-life have begun in earnest.

The highly introverted man, by the same token, may be caught out by his unconscious extroversion and find himself, for example, indulging in daydreams about feats of immense extroversion, such as changing history, overthrowing tyrants, fighting heroic battles, when in fact he is actually accomplishing nothing; that is, he daydreams his day away. Quite apart from such compensatory mechanisms, very few people are clearly on one or other side of this typology because it is complicated by the addition of what, in Jung's theory, are called the functions. Jung himself realised that if the distinction of extroversion-introversion was a valid basis for explaining the differences between Adler and Freud it was not, as it stood, an adequate basis for explaining the differences between himself and Adler, who, although quite clearly both introverts, had developed totally different theories. This led Jung on to the discovery and articulation of what has been termed the four functions.

THE FOUR FUNCTIONS

As a matter of empirical observation, we as human beings experience phenomena in four ways. That is, we orientate ourselves to the world in four ways or we take the world in, if you like, through four separate lenses. Perhaps the simplest and most direct way to demonstrate this is via a very concrete example. Imagine you are walking along the street and suddenly hear the loud shrieking of brakes. You look up and you see on the other side of the road a girl knocked off her bicycle by a car. You notice people are picking her up; a policeman arrives on the scene. Now these are the brute facts we take in through our senses. At the same time our thinking gets going and we begin to *think* that the girl was riding her bike across the side road out of which the car came and that the truck parked near the corner probably prevented the girl and the driver of the car from seeing each other. We also *think* that, judging by the amount of noise that the brakes made, the car must have been travelling fast.

At the same time we begin to make value judgements – such as, cars are a menace; something should be done to prevent licensed murder on the roads; happily the girl does not seem hurt; the driver doesn't seem to care at all.

Then the mind turns again, this time to a troubling possibility. You remember that somebody you know rides her bicycle home and you become concerned about her, telephone, and are relieved to know that she is all right. So, within a space of a few seconds, you have:

1. Perceived the facts; that is, taken in through your senses the event.
2. Thought about them and pieced them together logically by thinking about them.
3. Felt about them, made value judgements and given views; that is, felt about the situation.
4. You've looked beyond the facts to certain other possibilities, in this case as it happens not true, but for which you have used your intuition.

Now Plato, in his *Republic,* observed this fourfold character and referred to it as four facilities of the soul:

intelligence
demonstration
opinion
imagination

Galen, the ancient Greek physician, also discovered this fourfold temperament with his typology of:

melancholic (earth)
choleric (fire)
phlegmatic (water)
sanguine (air)

What Jung has done some twenty-three centuries after Plato is to independently come upon the same fourfold division. Jung called these four functions:

thinking
feeling
sensation
intuition

In short, they can be best seen as being like a compass or road map, with which we orientate ourselves to both the inner and outer world.

The remainder of this chapter will focus on each of these functions and then draw some very brief and altogether far too simplistic pictures of the various sorts of personalities that fall into each function.

Sensation

This is the function or mode of action by which we realise that a thing actually exists. It is perception through our senses. Sensation tells us that something is. It *does not* tell me what it is, and it does not tell me any other things about it. It only simply tells me that something is. So in our example it simply told us that an accident has happened; that is, we heard it and saw it, through the *senses* of hearing and seeing. In other situations we might taste and touch it. Sensation is to do with establishing that something exists through the senses.

Thinking

Thinking is the function by which one tells what things are. It adds a concept, because thinking is perception and judgement, thinking gives meaning and understanding. Thinking is a rational function. One makes logical judgements as to whether there is a connection between things or not. Thinking is the function that seeks to apprehend the world by thought, that is by logical inference and cognition. In our example we saw how thinking was used to work out the ways in which the accident might or might not have happened.

Feeling

Feeling is to do with values. It tells you whether a thing is acceptable, agreeable or not. It tells you what a thing is worth to you. It is the function that weighs and values. It is an evaluative function and therefore an entirely rational function, since it requires an act of judgement. For example, feels right, feels wrong; a rational, but not logical judgement.

Intuition

Intuition is fundamentally concerned with time. It is the function that tells us of future possibilities. It is the proverbial hunch and the function that informs us about the atmosphere that surrounds an experience or event. It is sometimes seen, and quite correctly so, as unconscious perception as opposed to sensation, which can be seen as conscious perception. Intuition is an irrational function, because the conclusions that are arrived at intuitively cannot easily be accounted for. Such conclusions literally come out of the blue and evidence cannot be given.

Now, just as individuals have introversion and extroversion, so also do humans constitutionally possess all four of these functions. But just as one or other of introversion or extroversion tends to predominate so also is it with the functions. When a reaction is a habitual one, then, and only then, may we accurately speak of a type. For example, there are people who obviously think more than others, who use thought in making decisions, judgements and solving problems, and who tend to regard thought as the most important attribute of human beings. Hence they tend to apply thinking, which they trust, to a whole host of situations, including ones where it is not necessarily the most appropriate function. When one uses a particular or specific function habitually, it is then termed the *superior function;* its opposite is then known as the *inferior function.* Thus, when one side or one function of the personality is over-emphasised, such as thinking, the feeling that is its opposite will be the inferior function and embedded in the unconscious.

A way of thinking about this is to think of the four functions as if they were four points of the compass. Immediately it becomes apparent that one cannot travel in a north and a south direction at the same time. Therefore north, if it is regarded as the equivalent of thinking, is the opposite direction from south, which could be regarded for the purpose of this example as feeling. However, as will be apparent from the compass analogy, one can indeed travel in a north-west direction, a north-east, or a south-west or a south-east direction. So also is it with the four functions and, whilst the present discussion has concentrated somewhat over-simplistically on the four basic

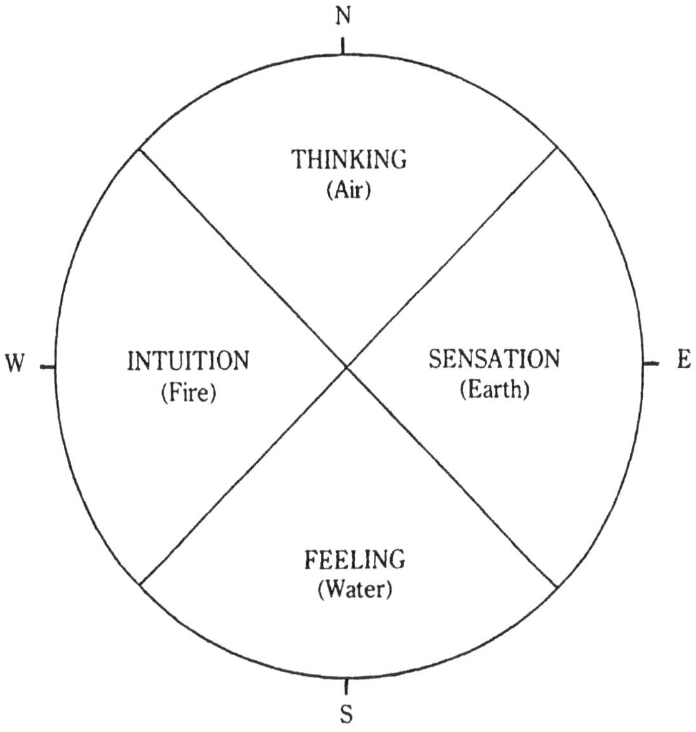

(N.B. Diagram shows THINKING as superior function, simply for purposes of convenience.)

functions, each individual, apart from having a superior function, also has, if you like, a north-west or north-east direction. That is, each individual also has what is termed an *auxiliary function.* This is the function that tends to aid and be the second major function that an individual uses. So, for example, one might come across what could be regarded as a thinking-sensation-type personality. This person would look at things with their senses and thinking rather than feeling and intuition. They would appraise and solve problems that they sense with their thinking apparatus. An example of such a person would be a scientist. However, rather than prolong the detailed explanation and example of each type, what follows are simple summaries of various types of individuals in which I have simply concentrated on the superior function and combined this with the attitude, whether it be extroverted or introverted.

TYPOLOGY OF INDIVIDUALS

Extroverted Thinking Type

Extroverted thinking types, if this is their superior function, tend to elevate objective thinking into the ruling passion of their lives. A classic example of such a type would be Darwin or Einstein. They tend to repress feelings and consequently behave in an impersonal, cool manner. Extroverted thinkers tend to use their thinking to run as much of the world as may be theirs to run. They have a well-developed capacity for organising facts, usually in advance, show a remarkable ability to define objectives and to move systematically towards completing these objectives. Through their reliance on their superior function of thinking they are logical, analytical, often critical, and tend to be swayed in their opinion only by reason. Whilst this has its positive factors, when a superior thinking type moves into a negative version, they tend to be, because of the repression of their feeling, autocratic, bigoted and on occasions quite vain. Furthermore, because feeling is their inferior or repressed function it can also disrupt them and explode into consciousness. So such extroverted thinking types are apt to experience very bad acting-out or temper-tantrum periods, since their feeling function has been repressed and therefore left in an immature psychological state.

Introverted Thinking Type

Just as the extroverted thinking type tends to reach out into the world, the introverted thinking types tend to use their superior function to analyse the world, but not to run it. Their energy, because of their introverted nature, is inwardly directed rather than outwardly directed, and such persons can be seen as being personified in the philosopher who seeks understanding of his own being and not necessarily the outside world. However, because thinking is still the superior function, such people, like their extroverted twins, tend to be logical, impersonal, objectively critical and not likely to be convinced or swayed in their opinion by anything other than logical reasoning. The negative aspects of such personality types tend to show up most readily in their personal relationships, where they are often emotionless and distant, and tend not to value people at all, but only ideas. As a rule the introverted thinking type is not particularly concerned, unlike the extroverted thinking type, with whether one likes his ideas or not. In the negative form he or she is inclined to be stubborn, stand-offish, prickly, arrogant and unapproachable. If the danger implicit in the extroverted thinking type is to be autocratic and bigoted, then the equivalent danger in the introverted thinking type is that they are in danger of having delusions of grandeur and becoming slowly but surely disconnected from the outer world, since introversion takes them on an inward, rather than outward, journey.

Extroverted Feeling Type

Extroverted feeling types are apt to be capricious, as feelings change as often as situations. They can be gushy, emotional, ostentatious and not infrequently moody. They develop strong attachments to people, but equally so are their attachments transitory and often of a short-term nature, for the extroverted feeling type can equally as quickly turn love into hate. They also tend to participate in the latest fads and fashions. The thinking function in the extroverted feeling type tends to be the inferior function, and therefore their thought processes are poorly developed. As a consequence, the extroverted feeling type, with their preoccupation concerning being attached to the outside world, tend to just go along with whatever is fashionable and show a remarkable absence of critical evaluation.

However, on a more positive note, extroverted feeling types usually radiate warmth and fellowship and their reliance on feeling as the superior function gives them a very personal approach to life, since feeling judges everything by personal values. Extroverted feeling types are exactly the type of personality you need at a party if you are worried about it not going properly. However, given that they are feeling types and extroverted, it tends to be difficult for them to face disagreeable facts or criticism that hurts. Because of this difficulty, extroverted feeling types show a tendency to sweep their problems under the rug instead of facing them and finding solutions, since thinking is usually the inferior function. In the occupational field, extroverted feeling types tend to do best at jobs where they deal with people and any situation where co-operation and good will are needed.

Introverted Feeling Type

Unlike their extroverted twin, introverted feeling types tend to keep their feelings hidden, are silent, inaccessible and often display melancholy or depression. They are taciturn, and also can give the impression of having inner harmony, seemingly some sort of mysterious charisma. What one often says of an introverted feeling type is 'still waters run deep'. Introverted feeling types judge the world by personal values. Being introverted, these values are not often shared. However, introverted feeling types tend to be idealists and measure their accomplishments against their internal standards of perfection, which can make life quite difficult for them. Introverted feeling types, given that they do not relate to the outer world well, can also suffer from grave feelings of self-doubt and internal standards that are quite unrealistic. Since thinking is quite often their inferior function, they can display an inability to critically evaluate situations in a logical manner and therefore can be easily swayed by charismatic leaders, often not stopping to question the quality of that leader.

Extroverted Sensation Type

This type is characterised by the accumulation of facts about the world. Extroverted sensation types tend to be realistic, practical, down-to-earth, and are often described as hard-headed. Extroverted sensation types are not particularly concerned about what things mean; in fact they are very often remarkably unreflective, and in the religious world would tend to be agnostic rather than belong to any religious organisation or set of religious beliefs.

Feelings in the extroverted sensation types are apt to be shallow, but seemingly, in contrast, their sexuality will be extremely strong because sensation types tend to have a strong relationship to their bodies. Indeed the physical world is the world in which extroverted sensation types feel most comfortable, since the extroversion takes them on the outside of themselves and sensation determines that they are more comfortable with their senses than with thinking or feeling. Their superior sensation may show itself in remarkable ability for understanding and handling machinery or materials for craft (for example, pottery), and also in an ability to recognise quality and line, texture, etc.

They also tend to have a well-developed capacity, as already mentioned, for the memory and ascertaining of exact factual information and very often show an ability to retain this. However, because feeling and intuition can often be their inferior function such extroverted sensation types can be, in the negative form, remarkably out of touch with the world of feelings, and therefore very insensitive and preoccupied with doing rather than being. So, under pressure, extroverted sensation types, when tense, are likely to take off into flights of fixing things on the outside of themselves rather than reflecting on the meaning of feelings on the inside of himself.

Introverted Sensation Type

Like all introverts, introverted sensation types stand aloof, since their psychic energy is directed inwards towards the inner world rather than out towards the outer reality. Very often the introverted sensation type can be preoccupied with inner sensations and can consider the outside world banal. The introverted sensation type may appear calm, a bit detached and even boring. Their sensation nature means that they do not tend to enter things impulsively and can be characterised by their painstaking, systematic and hard-working attention to detail and routine. However, once they do take on a task they tend to be hard to distract, discourage or stop.

Extroverted Intuitive Type

Extroverted intuitive types in the negative sense can be characterised by flightiness and instability and jumping from one situation to another, always looking for new worlds to conquer, very often before they have conquered the old worlds that they are currently in. They tend not to maintain an interest for very long, and the extroverted intuitive types are characterised by the fact that routine bores them very quickly. They have also been described as not being dependable as friends, again characteristic with their jumping from situation to situation, and their remarkable need to pick up numerous interests, but to drop them equally as quickly. On the positive side, nevertheless, the extroverted intuitive types can be remarkably enthusiastic innovators, always seeking new possibilities, new ways of doing things or quite new and fascinating things that might be done. Being intuitive as their superior function, they are characterised by a wealth of imagination and initiative and lots of impulsive energy. These are the sort of people that one would employ in an organisation because of their capacity for inspiration, but indeed their inability to stick at detail means that they are not as reliable in a position of overall direction or authority.

Introverted Intuitive Type

Introverted intuitive types are most clearly seen in the stereotype of the artist, the dreamer, the visionary, the prophet. They are often regarded as an enigma by their friends and very often regard themselves as being a misunderstood genius. Being intuitive and being introverted, there is no shortage of imaginative world and they tend therefore not to be in touch with external reality and are isolated within the inner images of their own internal world. However, on the positive side, because such introverted intuitive types are in touch with their inner images they tend to trust their visions and be able to develop new and exciting imaginary ideas regardless of established convention or popular belief. The eccentric is a classic introverted intuitive type. However, if sensation is lacking in their personality, the best of their ideas will tend to go to waste and be ignored, and themselves be regarded as eccentric cranks, unless in fact they can manage to put these visionary ideas into action.

It is important to note in reading these types that I have simply presented them in the most pure and distilled form and, indeed, in reality, people have various combinations of types as previously mentioned in terms of superior and auxiliary. The important task seems to me for each individual to try and identify what his superior function may be because in those situations in which he can use that, he will feel most comfortable and able to develop his strengths more readily. Identifying one's major type also allows one to be more sensitive and understanding of those situations in which we do feel most anxiety and in which we experience most conflict. This is simply because opposite types tend to irritate each other, and same types tend to be attracted to each other. More of this will become apparent in the section on marriage and personal development.

5. Self and the Individuation Process

It is clear from what has been written so far that, throughout his life, Jung was preoccupied with the reconciliation of the opposites within himself. Initially we encountered this struggle in his youthful conflict between his awkward Number One personality and his wise, old and learned Number Two personality. Later this became known or recognised as the struggle between his subjective and objective Self. Then, during Jung's work with schizophrenic patients, we saw another attempt to reconcile a need for such patients to have delusions on the one hand and the requirement on the other hand to relate to the outside world. In the previous chapter we discussed the encounters that Jung had with Freud and Adler, and how this led to his recognition of the opposite movement of psychic energy in the pattern of what Jung called extroversion and introversion. Finally, we discussed the opposites as constituted in the four functions of thinking, feeling, intuition and sensation. In relation to all these opposites, we discussed the law of compensation and the tendency within the psyche to redress any undue imbalance between consciousness and the unconscious mind. In other words, where one found a particular aspect of a person, whether it be a function (for example, thinking over-developed in consciousness) or a tendency towards do-gooding, then one found its opposite in the unconscious mind often personified in the form of a shadow figure that appeared in dreams or alternatively was projected onto other people.

Indeed, I think it fair to say that over and above all the things that Jungian psychology is, it is, in the final analysis, about the reconciliation of the opposites within us and the psychic energy that springs from its source in the tension between these opposites. This ought not to be a surprising assertion in so far as I think that the reconciliation and transcendence of opposites was the personal myth that moved Jung and, of course, connected him to the macrocosmic myth that is so characteristic of Eastern religious thought (that is, the transcendence of opposites leading to Nirvana or the conjunction of Atman and Brahman).

For Jung, in the simplest possible terms, this reconciliation of opposites and their integration resulting in transcendence is fundamentally achieved by bringing into consciousness the unconscious aspects of our being. This process is called *individuation* and the agent and the goal of this process is termed 'Self'. The process of individuation, as Jung said himself, is the central concept of his psychology. It is difficult at this point to know in which order to proceed, since the process of individuation and Self are inextricably bound together, and do not conform to some neat, logical, linear model of discussion. However, for purposes of making a beginning, I will start with Self, since it is both the agent and the means of individuation, and at the same time it is also paradoxically the goal. In so doing, I am reminded of the words of T. S. Eliot from one of his *Four Quartets,* 'Little Gidding':

> What we call the beginning is often the end
> And to make an end is to make a beginning
> The end is where we start from.

So also is it a beginning to discuss the Self; it is both the beginning and the end, for 'the end is where we start from'. Again, in the further words of Eliot from 'Little Gidding', one can see the process of Self when he says:

> We shall not cease from exploration
> And the end of all our exploring
> Will be to arrive where we started
> And know the place for the first time.

So let us start our exploring, and hopefully we also will arrive where we started from, since the essential quality of Self is that it is both the source and the goal, the beginning and the end. If this sounds paradoxical enough, then the penultimate paradox must be to try and talk about Self, which by its very nature is beyond words and transcends thinking. Hence one is forced to rely on metaphors of Self, on poetry, on mythology and symbols (that is, manifestations of Self). For this reason I again turn to T. S. Eliot, who I feel provides an exquisite description of Self in his poem 'Burnt Norton':

> At the still point of the turning world. Neither flesh nor fleshless;
> Neither from nor towards; at the still point, there the dance is,
> But neither arrest nor movement. And do not call it fixity,
> Where past and future are gathered. Neither movement from nor towards,
> Neither ascent nor decline. Except for the point, the still point,
> There would be no dance, and there is only the dance.

This is, to my mind, exactly the same as Jung's definition of Self, although expressed in poetic imagery. Jung, in his volume entitled *Psychology and Alchemy,* said this of Self:

It is not only the centre but also the whole circumference which embraces both consciousness and unconsciousness; it is the centre of this totality, just as the ego is the centre of the conscious mind. (*CW* 12:41)

Again in the *Two Essays on Analytical Psychology:*

The Self is our life's goal, for it is the completest expression of that fateful combination we call individuality. (*CW* 7:238)

It *is,* as Eliot would say, the 'dance, and there is only the dance'.

Marie-Louise von Franz, a longstanding collaborator of Jung's, in her description of Self captures the immortality theme. In discussing the goal of Self, she had this to say:

The goal of individuation, as pictured in unconscious images, represents a kind of mid-point or centre in which the supreme value and the greatest life intensity are concentrated. It cannot be distinguished from the images of the supreme value of various religions.*

With respect to experiencing Self, Marie-Louise von Franz goes on to say:

*Marie-Louise von Franz, *Carl Gustav Jung: his myth in our time,* Little, Brown & Co., 1975, p. 73.

The experience of Self brings a feeling of standing on solid ground inside oneself, on a patch of eternity, which even physical death cannot touch.*

Here we see reference to the immortal or divine aspects of Self, which I think make it plausible to relate the Jungian concept of Self to the Christian idea of Soul. In this sense then, Christ being crucified to redeem us from our sins can be seen alternatively as the archetypal expression of the redemption of Self from the darkness of the unconscious, since, as we saw in the discussion of the 'Two Travellers', crucifixion of the ego may be the necessary condition for the redemption of Self. That is, suffering resulting in the need to change a particular conscious aspect of our being may be the necessary condition for change. In this sense, for me, life is a process of the redemption of Self from the abyss of the unconscious, a process personified in Christ's crucifixion and institutionalised to the point of sterility in organised Christianity! It is perhaps the death of this Christian myth through the aegis of rigid, organised and institutionalised religion that drove Jung to restate the redemptive process in psychological terms. So long as Self is projected or maintained on Christ being crucified on the cross, we cannot discover our inner Self and the need for an internal crucifixion of various conscious attitudes. What then, in psychological terms, is Self that has to be redeemed?

As has already been mentioned, *wholeness* is the goal of the psyche, but this does not occur by chance or some random ordering of the psyche's contents. On

*Ibid. p. 74.

the contrary it is organised by the archetype we have termed Self. Hence this Self is often termed, as already mentioned, the archetype of order, that archetypal pattern, or energy to integrate, to move towards a state of psychological completeness or wholeness. The Self is the central archetype in the collective unconscious, the prime mover if you like, the sun of the psyche solar system. It draws to itself like a magnet all the separate parts of the psyche; archetypes, complexes, shadows, etc., and unites the personality, giving one that sense of standing on solid ground that von Franz talks of, giving one a sense of 'oneness' and harmony within himself or herself and with the world.

The Self archetype can be described in psychological terms as an inner guiding factor, and one can experience the expression of this Self in quite meditative moments; for example, as an inner voice. It is the mid-point and integrative point between the two worlds of consciousness and the unconscious. Having struggled with the dark side of our nature and accepted our shadow aspects, followed by making conscious the opposite sex function within us (the anima-animus), we are then as a rule ready to begin the arduous task of reconciling and integrating the opposites within us, the archetypal image of this unification, the mid-point common to both consciousness and unconsciousness is the Self. It is, so to speak, the last station on the path to self-realisation, the emergence of which is most clearly seen in its completed form in such religious figures as the Buddha or Christ. But in saying this I am also alerting you to the fact that few mere mortals are ever going to achieve such a state of psychological development, but the process of striving for it, driven by Self, is inevitable and intrinsic to human nature as is breathing and eating to the physiological world. As Soren Kierkegaard said: 'To become oneself is man's true vocation.'

In the present times my personal view is that there is an ever-increasing tendency to pursue 'self-realisation' without struggling with the more painful task of self-knowledge. The proliferation of instant gurus has facilitated the defensive fantasy that self-realisation is possible without self-knowledge. All that is in fact achieved by such instant and painless 'self-realisation' is a persona of self-realisation, a mask or ego-image of it, but not a psychic reality. Hence the first real stress or upset that occurs to such people with a persona of self-realisation sees that so-called realisation crumble into depression or explode into anger. The Jungian viewpoint is unequivocally that self-knowledge is the path to self-realisation, and in this sense it belongs to the ancient paths as exemplified in such traditions as Buddhism.

The archetypal image of this reconciliation of opposites, of this emergence of Self, of this transformation of opposites into a higher synthesis is called the uniting symbol, of which the most eloquent example is the mandala; but in saying this I am not wishing to imply in any way that it is the only symbol, as there are indeed many such symbols of unity. Some brief examples are the tree, fish, a child, a hermaphroditic figure (an obvious symbol of completeness), a jewel, a flower, a chalice (as, for example, in the Arthurian legend of the search for the Holy Grail).

We have already briefly touched on mandalas in discussing the archetypes. Mandala is a Sanskrit word meaning magic circle, and its symbolism includes all concentrically arranged figures, all circles or squares arranged with a central point and divided into four or some combination of four. It is one of the oldest religious symbols (the earliest form perhaps being the sun wheel) and is found throughout the world and in various religions, which attests to its true universal and thereby collective unconscious qualities. A classic Christian mandala is Christ and the four evangelists as shown, for example, in the Book of Kells, or indeed Christ himself on the Cross. It is a regular and ritualistic symbol in Eastern religions. However, regardless of whatever form a mandala takes, it is always a symbol of unity, a symbol of Self, a symbol of wholeness; a symbol of the goal of individuation.

INDIVIDUATION

The task of completing oneself, of moving towards the experience of Self, is in Jung's terms called individuation. There is no wholeness without a recognition of opposites within, and this process of recognition, this process of truly becoming an individual, is termed individuation. The first thing to realise about individuation is that it is essentially a process that takes place most obviously in the second half of life, and this will be very much the focus of the next two sections on anima/animus and the mid-life transition. In Jung's view the process is stimulated when consciousness, including the development of the superior function into consciousness, has reached that point or degree of development when it has diverged too far from the unconscious. Another way of saying this is when a split or disconnection occurs or exists between consciousness and unconsciousness due to the lopsided and/or uneven development of the conscious aspects of the personality, or the superior function. Hence the individuation process does not seem to get going in earnest, on average, until the second half of life, and is most clearly seen in successful individuals experiencing difficulties at the mid-point in their lives that elsewhere I have called the mid-life crisis.*

In precise psychological terms, individuation represents the process of differentiation, of the bringing into consciousness of the shadow figures and the clear differentiation between Self and the other, based on self-knowledge and not projection. Individuation can be seen as the process of withdrawing projections and accepting what we previously thought was somebody else's failings or strengths as our own, and then recognising that the true Self is both individual and universal. The peculiar paradox, it seems to me, of becoming an individual through the process of individuation is that it facilitates belonging to the whole and the universal by recognising what is unique in each of us and yet paradoxically at the same time shared; the recognition of the relationship between the microcosmic and the macrocosmic worlds.

In fact, the conscious attitude that accompanies the achievement of a level of individuation is essentially one of acceptance, of ceasing either to do violence to one's own nature by repressing it and/or to do violence to somebody else's nature by projecting our own unconscious onto it. In his commentary on *The Secret*

*Peter O'Connor, *Understanding the Mid-Life Crisis*, Sun Books, 1981.

of the Golden Flower; an ancient oriental meditative text, translated by Richard Wilhelm, through whom Jung was first introduced to the idea of individuation, Jung quotes a letter from a former patient which, I think, captures the essential quality of an individual who is in the process of being individuated.

> Out of the evil much good has come to me. By keeping quiet, repressing nothing, remaining attentive and by accepting reality – taking things as they are and not as I want them to be – by doing all this unusual knowledge has come to me and unusual powers as well, such as I could never have imagined before. I always thought that when we accepted things they overpowered us in some way or other. This turns out not to be true at all, and it is only by accepting them that one can assume an attitude toward them. So now I intend to play the game of life, being receptive to whatever comes to me, good and bad, sun and shadow, forever alternating and, in this way, also accepting my own nature with its positive and negative sides. Thus everything becomes more alive to me. What a fool I was! How I tried to force everything to go according to the way I thought it ought to.*

In summary, then, individuation is the process by which a person becomes a psychological individual; that is, a separate, indivisible, unity or whole. The mechanics of this process is the task of bringing into consciousness the unconscious contents of the mind (that is, self-awareness), thereby facilitating their

* *The Secret of the Golden Flower,* translated by Richard Wilhelm, Routledge & Kegan Paul, 1975, p. 126.

differentiation and ultimately their integration. As Jung said in relation to individuation: 'Consciousness and unconsciousness do not make a whole when one of them is suppressed and injured by the other.'*

As I have already stated, there is no wholeness without a recognition of the opposites, and thus the first step in individuation, which usually begins around the mid-life period, is the confrontation with one's shadow figures. You will perhaps recall that in the previous chapter, when I quoted Jung as saying that confronting the shadow requires courage, since one of the consequences is that a man or a woman comes to the realisation that whatever is wrong in the world is in himself or herself, and as such a man or woman has saddled himself or herself with new problems. The second stage of individuation or the pathway towards integration and the experience of Self is characterised by encounters with the 'Soul image', the contrasexual elements within ourselves, which Jung has termed anima and animus.

As this is the focus of the next chapter, I will not go into detail here, other than to say that every man has an Eve within him and every woman an Adam. Such contrasexual or opposite sex aspects of our psyche are both archetypal and personal. Like the shadow figures, we usually first encounter them via projections onto someone else of the opposite sex, resulting in an attachment and powerful attraction to them. We also encounter the anima or animus, the contrasexual components within ourselves, in dreams, fantasies and visions. It is by bringing it into conscious-

**Archetypes and the Collective Unconscious*, volume 9, part 1 of *CW*, p. 228.

ness that we differentiate it out from the unconscious and thereby render the opposite sex elements within ourselves available for integration, thus moving one step further towards wholeness. The final step brings us back the full circle to the integration of opposites and brings often the intolerable tension of the opposites as part of the process of experiencing the Self or deep centre within our being. It is in the transcendence of opposites via their integration, the internal recognition and acceptance that we are composed of opposites, that results in the true experience of Self. It is in this experience that an individual's centre of psychic gravity shifts from the ego to the true centre of his being, to – in the words of T. S. Eliot – where the dance is. In other words, to that spot in the psyche that is a non-personal and not exclusively personal centre – the Self – where the individual microcosmic psyche is connected to the macrocosmic, where Atman and Brahman are united, where what is above is also below.

6. Alchemy

Jung's rediscovery of alchemy and his prolonged period of work on it cannot be separated from his early period of professional and personal development despite the fact that Jung himself was in his early fifties when he first began his serious study of alchemy.

After the separation from Freud in 1912, Jung began his profound experiment on and in himself. The primary technique he used appears to have been active imagination, which is the name of the technique used for exploring the unconscious mind. In the simplest possible terms, active imagination is akin to conscious daydreaming, really entering a fantasy and following it through to its completion. Sometimes active imagination takes the form of writing (which is obviously what Jung did a lot of), painting, sculpting, dancing or even talking out loud to oneself. In short, active imagination is simply giving form, giving expression in outer reality, of an inner image or reality or series of images that enter the mind following an initial period of having emptied the mind from the trains of conscious thought. The final step in active imagination is what Jungians call the ethical confrontation; that is, taking seriously the content of the active imagination and earnestly seeking its meaning and not simply dismissing it as 'mere fantasy', which is the usual means of dealing with an outcome we do not consciously like.

This self-imposed experimental phase of Jung's, much of which is contained in what is termed the 'Red

Book', began in 1912 and lasted approximately until 1919. It was a period that can be best regarded as a pioneering work in the jungle of the unconscious mind. Whilst these years had the effect of isolating Jung from his colleagues and the scientific and professional worlds, he nevertheless regarded these years as the most important in his life, since it was during these years that he confronted his unconscious. He explored it and came to a profoundly deep understanding of it, which had the effect of indelibly altering Jung himself as a person; that is, it had a transformation effect. This effect, interestingly enough, is the exact effect that has been described as occurring in ancient shamans or primitive medicine men following what has been termed an 'initiatory illness' (a period not unrelated to the mid-life crisis transition). However, it was to be some twenty years beyond the beginning of this self-imposed experiment before Jung was able to understand in some measure the products of his active imagination that he had so assiduously and conscientiously recorded in his Red Book. In his autobiography he says:

> First I had to find evidence for the historical prefiguration of my inner experiences. That is to say, I had to ask myself 'where have my particular premises already occurred in history'? If I had not succeeded in finding such evidence, I would never have been able to substantiate my ideas. Therefore my encounter with alchemy was decisive for me, as it provided me with the historical basis which I had hitherto lacked. (*MDR* 200)

This quotation, I feel, brings home a point often overlooked in relation to Jung; that he, like other people, wanted to find support and justification for his ideas, particularly given their personal nature. Jung was, no doubt, left wondering whether other people, perhaps at other times in history, had felt or experienced what he had experienced over that period of intensive self-analysis and the subsequent years. As he stated himself in his Foreword to Richard Wilhelm's *The Secret of the Golden Flower* (a book, incidentally, that was the turning-point in Jung's pursuit of alchemy):

My results based on fifteen years of effort seemed inconclusive because no possibility of comparison offered itself. I knew of no realm of human experience with which I might have backed up my findings with some degree of assurance. (p. xiii)

However, as we have seen so often in this discussion, Jung's professional and personal lives, his being and his theories, are inextricably bound together, the last constituting an attempt to explain and give meaning and order to the former. Also, as we have said before, specifically in relation to Jung's discovery of the collective unconscious, ideas often announced themselves in dreams to Jung long before he had been able to attempt any conscious conceptual elaboration of his ideas.

His introduction to alchemy conforms exactly to this pattern of discovery: 'Before I discovered alchemy, I had a series of dreams which repeatedly dealt with the same theme' (*MDR* 193). This theme was as follows:

Beside my house stood another, that is to say, another wing or annex, which was strange to me and each time

I wondered in my dream why I did not know this house, although it had apparently always been there. Finally came a dream in which I reached the other wing. I discovered there a wonderful library dating largely from the sixteenth and seventeenth centuries. Large, fat, folio volumes bound in pigskin stood along the wall. Among them were a number of books embellished with copper engravings of a strange character, and illustrations containing curious symbols such as I had never seen before. At the time I did not know to what they referred; only much later did I recognise them as alchemical symbols. (*MDR* 193-4)

Jung goes on to make some brief interpretive comments about this dream in which he says the 'unknown wing of the house' was a part of his own personality, a part of him of which he was not yet conscious, and the library obviously referred to alchemy. Interestingly enough, some fifteen years after this series of dreams, Jung had assembled a library very much like the one in this actual dream. It is still housed today in his home in Zürich and comprises probably the finest and most complete private alchemical library in the world. However, it was a crucial dream of Jung's in 1926, a year approximately after the preceding dream, that anticipated Jung's encounter with alchemy. The dream is as follows:

I was in the South Tyrol. It was wartime. I was on the Italian front and driving back from the frontline with a little man, a peasant, in his horse-drawn wagon. All around us shells were exploding, and I knew we had to push on as quickly as possible for it was very dangerous. We had to cross a bridge and then go through a tunnel whose vaulting had been partially destroyed by the shells. Arriving at the end of the tunnel, we saw before us a sunny landscape and I recognised it as the region round Verona. Below me lay the city, radiant in full sunlight. I felt relieved and we drove on out into the green, thriving Lombard plain. The road led through lovely springtime countryside; we saw the rice fields, the olive trees and the vineyards. Then diagonally across the road I caught sight of a large building, a manor house of grand proportions, rather like the palace of a North Italian duke. It was a typical manor house with many annexes and outbuildings. Just as at the Louvre, the road led through a large courtyard and past the palace. The little coachman and myself drove in through a gate, and from here we could see , through a second gate at the far end, the sunlit landscape again. I looked round; to my right was the façade of the manor house, to my left the servants' quarters and the stables, barns and other outbuildings which stretched on for a long way.

Just as we reached the middle of the courtyard, in front of the main entrance, something unexpected happened; with a dull clang, both gates flew shut. The peasant leaped from his seat and exclaimed – 'now we are caught in the seventeenth century'. Resignedly I thought, 'well that's that, but what is there to do about it? Now we shall be caught for years'. Then the consoling thought came to me, 'someday, years from now, I shall get out again'. (*MDR* 194)

This is a very rich and dramatic dream full of extremely rich symbolism. The shells, for example,

Jung interpreted as missiles coming from the 'other side'; that is, the unconscious mind. I think the peasant can be seen as the practical, earthy, purposeful part of Jung, systematically but slowly leading him back to alchemy. Interestingly enough they are going back from the front line, that is back in time perhaps away from the conscious mind of present day. There is also, it seems to me, several symbols of renewal in this journey; back through lovely springtime suggests that retreating from conscious position (present time) will have the effect of renewal of the spirit (that is, new growth). The manor house on the right (that is, consciousness) is a façade, which I feel reflects Jung's anxiety at not having any comparative evidence to back up his theories. Interestingly, the buildings on the left are very real – stables, barns, etc. – and these to my mind refer to working buildings and storehouses of food, symbolically representing the things to be found in the unconscious mind.

Subsequently, Jung found himself reading 'ponderous tomes' on religion and philosophy and some on alchemy, without enlightenment. He states that at this time, 'I regarded alchemy as something off the beaten track . . . rather silly' (*MDR* 195). The critical turning-point was the book I have already mentioned: Richard Wilhelm's translation of the ancient Chinese alchemical text entitled *The Secret of the Golden Flower*. Wilhelm sent this book to Jung with the request that he write a commentary on the text. This was in 1928, two years after the dream of being locked in the seventeenth century. Jung's response to the text, the origins of which went back to the Tang Dynasty (eighth century), was as follows:

I devoured the manuscript at once, for the text gave me undreamed of confirmation of my ideas about the mandala and the circumambulation of the centre. That was the first event that broke through my isolation. I became aware of an affinity; I could establish ties with something and someone. (*MDR* 197)

These last words are to my mind very revealing of the human side of Jung, who at fifty-three years of age, despite much respectable professional success behind him, was still feeling the acute aloneness that was so characteristic of his adolescence. This book aroused Jung's interest in alchemy, and to his surprise he found other parallels to his work, particularly the internal work, the self-imposed analysis; that is, confirmation for those arduous and presumably tortuous years following the break with Freud. For example, he found a direct parallel between his discovery of the mandala symbolism in his patients and the Chinese concept in *The Secret of the Golden Flower* of the 'circulation of light'. Here, too, in this very ancient text, the circular movement was intended to set in motion a development of personality leading to individuation. Here, also, was the symbol of Self, of unity, of self-realisation.

A further analogy was found in the two concepts of Soul that are discussed in the *Golden Flower*. In this text they are personified by the masculine 'cloud demon' Hun, and the feminine earthbound 'white ghost' P'o, which exactly parallel Jung's concepts of anima and animus. Further, the meditative process spelt out in the *Golden Flower* paralleled the same sort of psychic trransformation that Jung himself had experienced and had later come to conceptualise as individuation. Thus, with his appetite whetted, he pursued the exploration of alchemy, and was soon to discover that here, too, the art was about producing the incorruptible stone, the Self, or the *lapis philosophorum.*

Although Jung started his alchemical studies in earnest from this time on, that is 1928, it was not until seven years later (seven equalling one spiritual year!) that he represented his findings to the public for the first time at what was then termed the Eranos meetings in Ascona, Switzerland. However, it was a further seven years, 1942 (originally published in 1944), before these lectures given at Eranos were elaborated into one of Jung's key works, entitled *Psychology and Alchemy,* which forms volume 12 of his *Collected Works.*

Well, let us now turn to alchemy and briefly discuss what it is and how such a seemingly irrelevant and esoteric art was able to provide Jung with the much needed confirmation and validation of his own views. On the surface, alchemy appears as a fairly unlikely source of such confirmation, since normally it is equated with superstitious nonsense in which cranks thought they could make gold through a process of pseudo-chemical procedure. In a more objective sense, alchemy is regarded not just as the hobby of crackpots, but as the genuine predecessor of modern chemistry. It is certainly true that alchemists did try to make gold, but what is not commonly appreciated is that for some of the alchemists, in their own words, *aurum nostrum non est aurum vulgi*; that is, 'our gold is not the common gold'.

To understand this, we shall have to trace the outline of the history of alchemy. Its earliest origins appear to have been separately in Egypt and China. The Egyptian origins are supported by references to various gods, in particular Hermes (Thoth), who was associated with late mediaeval alchemy in the form of the god Mercury (romanised version of Hermes). Chinese origins, as we have already seen, are evident in such early manuscripts as *The Secret of the Golden Flower*, but some evidence of alchemical knowledge exists as early as the fifth century BC in China. Gold, or the making of it, was present in both civilisations. Then there came a Greek-Egyptian era – including the alchemical theories of Plato and Aristotle, focusing primarily on the four elements of fire, air, water and earth. In fact, one alchemical writer, Hopkins, has argued that alchemy as it came to be known from the thirteenth through to the seventeenth centuries in Europe was indeed the child of Greek philosophy.* I suspect that the central basis of this assertion is that Aristotle held that *all* bodies were composed of the four elements, just in differing proportions. Therefore, as a direct corollary of this, one body could be changed or transmuted into the other; for example, water could become air (steam) by simply heating it.

Alongside this belief, in the possibility of all matter potentially capable of being transmuted into another form, was a second belief or assumption that proves to be central to the understanding of alchemy, and that is that all matter was like man, alive and sensitive and having a spirit or life within it just as man (that is, there was no clear distinction between man and matter). A

*A. J. Hopkins, *Alchemy, Child of Greek Philosophy*, Columbia University Press, 1934.

direct consequence of this belief was the further belief that all matter, just like man, had within it, or him, the potential to be perfect, and that the agent of this process was spirit or pneuma. Such spirit can be seen as having the power to change base metals into their perfected form, that being personified or symbolised by 'gold'; hence the alchemist dictum *aurum nostrum non est aurum vulgi.*

Thus it makes very good sense that later alchemists believed in the possibility of changing base metals such as copper into gold, since all things, from their point of view, could be changed into all other things simply because all substances were fundamentally composed of the same four basic elements. And secondly, like man, matter had the potential for perfect form within itself. All that was required was a suitable agent for bringing about this transmutation and redeeming the perfect matter, 'gold', from the base metal.

This redeeming or transmuting agent became known under a wide range of terms, and one can see constant reference to it in Jung, from such terms as the *lapis*, philosopher's stone, *lapis philosophorum, lapis invisibilitatis, mercurius* or the philosopher's gold. In searching for this stone, the alchemist was endeavouring to liberate the spirit he believed to be concealed in matter; that is, to redeem the divine spirit, the perfect form, from the vessel of matter in which it was held captive.

This stone, this spirit, or whatever other name it goes by, is both the starting-point and the goal of the alchemical opus or work, regardless of whatever stage of alchemy one is talking about. It is in this very sentence of the stone being the starting-point and the goal as well as the transmuting agent or agent of change, that one can immediately see the link that so excited Jung between his theories and alchemy. The direct link is simply that the stone, the *lapis*, the philosopher's gold, etc., is equivalent to the Self, since both are the starting-point, the agent and the goal of the opus, whether that opus or work be alchemical or psychological.

That the stone, the mystical transmuting agent, should be known as a stone in fact related back to Jung's very early life as a schoolboy, when he liked to play outdoors, particularly along the garden wall of his parent's home where there was a slope and, embedded in this slope, a stone, 'my stone' as Jung called it. He says of it:

> Often when I was alone I sat down on this stone and then began an imaginary game that went something like this . . . 'I am sitting on top of this stone and it is underneath'. But the stone could also say, 'I' and think 'I am lying here on this slope and he is sitting on top of me'. The question arose 'am I the one who is sitting on the stone, or am I the stone on which he is sitting'. (*MDR* 331)

Here we see in this ten-year-old mind of Jung the archetypal recognition of Self being the equivalent of stone or alternatively as Self being represented by stone in the outer world. Closer to home we can still recognise this powerful link amongst the Australian Aboriginals with their Churinga stone, which they believe has the magic life forces residing in it. A contemporary cinematic expression of this Aboriginal myth can be seen in Peter Weir's film *The Last Wave*. The stone therefore appears to be an age-old symbol for the eternal, the enduring in man, the immortal – the Self. That the alchemist believed that this stone could be produced or liberated from matter in which it was concealed was entirely consistent, as we have already seen, with the lack of any distinction between mind and matter. Such a distinction appears to have come into existence with any clarity only in the latter part of the seventeenth century with the evolution of the subjective and objective worlds as personified and exemplified in Descartes's *Principles of Natural Philosophy*.

However, in pragmatic terms, what this lack of distinction between mind and matter, this Aristotelian principle of unity of matter, meant was that the alchemist drew no conscious distinction between the contents of their mind and the matter that they were experimenting on or with. Thus what they experienced as properties of matter was at the same time the content of their own unconscious mind. The chemical experiments simply paralleled an unconscious psychological experiment for the perfection of their own internal being. That is, the liberation of the 'gold' within themselves as personified and explicated in the liberation of gold from matter. In the alchemical symbolism, what Jung was able to discover was that the stages and the images were of an inner transformation process expressing itself in pseudo-chemical language. Hence the stone, the *lapis*, that the alchemists were trying to liberate from its vessel of matter, was the Self. That is, they were trying to liberate the Self from the chaos and the darkness of the primitive matter of their unconscious mind.

It was both things in a parallel way, so alchemy was indeed the precursor of chemistry, since it seems that they did do actual chemical experiments and developed certain fundamental chemical knowledge. But at the same time, because there was no distinction between mind and matter, it was, and is in my view, the precursor of depth psychology, in particular Jungian psychology. Thus the opus or work of the alchemist provides in an outside, externalised, projected and thereby totally unconscious form a picture of the work, the difficulties, the dangers and the rewards of the process of individuation. It is as if it is an outside language for an internal process, and Jung needed this historical link to validate what up until then had been his personal and subjective views.

Thus alchemy provided the illuminating parallel to the individuation process. As products of their times and cultural environments, alchemy and the individuation process differ greatly. But what both have in common, regardless of time and cultural differences, is that they are attempts to lead man to self-realisation. Hence the language of alchemy has to be read in *both* its exoteric form (that is, as a primitive and simplistic chemical language) *and* in its esoteric or mystical form as a symbolic language for the development of Self, that is the individuation process. The making of gold is the making of Self, the Soul-making that we discussed previously. In this sense, as Jung says in the Preface to a catalogue of alchemical books issued by the antiquarian bookseller Kelvin Andrew Zeigler of Zürich: 'Consequently alchemy gains the quite new and interesting aspect of a projected psychology of the collective unconscious and thus ranks with mythology and folklore.'

In discussing alchemy it is also important to take note of Jung's view that alchemy as such existed in a compensatory relationship throughout the Middle Ages and mediaeval periods to orthodox Christianity. Since, within the orthodox view, it was man who needed to be redeemed, but within the alchemical model it is God, the perfect form, hidden and contained in matter, that needed to be redeemed by man. In this sense we can once again see the law of compensation, or the law of balance operating within the psyche of man; alchemy providing the compensatory view to the consciously held one of redemption.

The alchemist undertook this task of redeeming, from what was termed the primitive material, the first material, or *massa confusa*, the chaos, the spirit that was imprisoned in it. The production stage by stage of the alchemical 'treasure' corresponds therefore to the deliverance or bringing to consciousness of the Self, from the darkness and primitive chaos of the unconscious mind. That it, alchemy, stood in a compensatory relationship to Christianity can be seen in Jung's statement that:

> The Christian opus is an operari in honour of God the Redeemer undertaken by man who stands in need of redemption, while the alchemical opus is the labour of Man the Redeemer in the cause of the divine world Soul slumbering and awaiting redemption in matter.*

*'Relations Between Ego and the Unconscious', *CW* 12:456-7.

Hence this represents the antithesis or the opposite of the Christian belief system, that God redeemed man; and thus the alchemists were apt to be persecuted by the Christian church, and this has been given in some places as one possible reason why even the enlightened alchemists, who seemingly knew what they were on about was not chemistry exclusively, but a mystical journey, continued to use chemical language as a means of avoiding persecution. The notion of redemption also related to the previous chapter, where I pointed out that Jung, in my opinion, has restated the redemptive process in psychological terms, substantiated by alchemy, and rescued redemption from the institutionalised sterility of organised Christianity; that is, from its lopsided consciousness.

Where one can see that the ancient alchemist projected the problems of redemption into matter, along with the projection of good, bad, dark and light, modern man can be seen as having projected the problem of redemption onto 'God' (aided and abetted by orthodox Christianity) and good and evil onto other people or nations. Hence the work remains the same; alchemy merely gives us an objectified account of redeeming the perfect form within ourselves.

ALCHEMICAL STAGES

Although the alchemical texts show many variations and indeed are very complex, there appears to be general agreement that the philosopher's stone or philosopher's gold is produced in three stages:

1. Nigredo: darkness or blackening.
2. Albedo: whiteness or whitening.
3. Rubedo: reddening or colouring of gold.

Nigredo

The work began with what has been termed the *mass confusa* or *prima materia*, which in actual matter form was often composed of four common base metals, in particular, lead, tin, copper and iron. If these are, for the moment, seen in a slightly broader context and related to the astrological view of the world, which can be considered as pre-dating the alchemical view, then one can immediately see an interesting relationship in so far as Saturn represents lead, the metal of Jupiter is tin, of Venus is copper and of Mars is iron. Taken one step farther, symbolically Saturn represents limitation, whereby Jupiter represents expansion and hence a pair of opposites. Venus represents love and Mars aggression, another pair of opposites. So in fact at this stage, if you like, the beginning of the black mass is a pair of opposites, and thereby is highly symbolic of man's psyche. The opposites are all mixed up and producing a black mass, that is an undifferentiated, disintegrated, unconscious mind. Hence what happens in the nigredo phase is that this black mass, this *prima materia,* is first *calcinated.* Within this process the alchemist simply heated the material, the basic metals, that symbolically we now see as being composed of the opposites of expansion and limitation and love and aggression to reduce it to a state of fine powder. The next stage of the alchemist's process was that it was then *putrefied.* That is, the calcinated material that had been reduced to a state of fine powder was separated out into an inert mass. This was followed by a form of washing, sometimes called solution, involving or resulting in the purification of matter. Finally in this nigredo phase comes the *distillation* process. This consists of boiling the liquid and reconverting the vapour into a liquid again by cooling it. This phase has sometimes also been referred to in the alchemical literature as 'the rain of purified matter'.

Alchemists referred to this nigredo or blackening phase as a dangerous stage in which poisonous vapours often could develop. Lead or quick silver (mercury) poisoning could occur, as also could explosions, since all of this took place in a retort or furnace. According to the old text, there lives in lead 'an impudent demon who can cause a sickness of the spirit or lunacy'. This nigredo phase has its psychological parallel, its 'internal parallel', in the first stage of individuation, that is the integration of the shadow and the recognition of the opposites within us. At this stage there usually exists in the beginning only a black mass, a mass of confusion with all the opposites mixed up, half of them projected onto other people and the shadow aspects of Self quite often disowned. The calcination that occurred in the physical world in matter can be seen as occurring symbolically or internally as a heating up and transforming of the shadow through emotion. That is, it is only when we find ourselves repeatedly having emotional outbursts with others, heating ourselves up so to speak psychologically, that we first have cause to reflect upon what it is within us that drives us to such behaviour. We know from a previous chapter that it is the shadow aspect, or the darkness within. The putrefication that occurred in the physical world can then be seen psychologically as the beginning of separating these black or shadow aspects out from each other, the beginning recognition, if you prefer, of them psychologically as a prelude to their integration. The final steps in the nigredo phase of solution and distillation are refinements of the shadow, the cleansing via the process of bringing them into consciousness and recognising them, thereby washing them clean from the darkness of the unconscious mind and the projection of them onto other people.

However, as the old alchemists pointed out, this nigredo phase, this working on the dark shadow aspects of Self, on the black mass within ourselves, has implicit in it certain dangers. The most prevalent one, alchemically speaking now, appears to find its origins in the 'impudent demon that lives in lead'. Translated psychologically or symbolically, one can take this to mean depression. Since what we know from the literature of symbolism is that lead is equated with Saturn, and Saturn with limitation, and it is often acquainted with a depressive or leaden feeling. In fact, one often says of people who are depressed that they feel weighted down. This makes sense psychologically and clinically, since when a person begins in therapy to recognise their shadow aspects, to start to withdraw some of their dark side of their personality, there is often a depressive reaction; that is, the 'impudent demon' causes a sickness of the spirit or psyche. A simple explanation of this is, as we have already seen, the withdrawal of projections, the bringing back from the outside world the parts of ourselves that were previously disowned and put onto other people. This process can very often leave people with a painful and at times depressing feeling that whatever is wrong with the world or others is actually wrong in themselves. For some individuals this results in a shattering of self-illusions that can create in its wake a feeling of having lived a totally phony and hypocritical life, and hence they can feel much despair about themselves and therapy. We can see in this a direct parallel to Jung's own life in that period between 1912 and 1919, when he explored in depth his own shadow side and had many and prolonged, depressive experiences.

Albedo

The second stage, as already indicated, is the albedo or whitening phase. In the alchemical work the nigredo was usually followed by the albedo phase or stage. Here the main operation was nowhere near as strenuous as the nigredo and consisted mainly of regulating the heat in the retort stand in the outer world, and keeping it at an even and regular temperature, making sure that it was neither over-heating the material, which would result in drying it up, or under-heating it, thus allowing the ingredients to cool down too much and to return to the basic black mass. Psychologically the albedo or whitening phase represents the first transmutation and integration of the inner contrasexual components, the anima in the man and the animus in the woman.

This inner union of opposites, this marriage between opposites, is called in alchemy the *hieros gamos* or sometimes referred to as the 'mystical marriage' or alternatively the 'chymical marriage'. In essence it is , I believe, not just the union of the contrasexual components, but also the beginning of the union and ultimately the transcendence of all the opposites within us. The contrasexual union, the union of anima and animus, in the albedo phase is in my view the prototype of the union of opposites that is to follow. It is,

I suspect, the psychological parallel to the albedo phase that is at the basis of so many marital problems when couples in which anima and animus are respectively activated; and people often characterised by a simultaneous attraction and hatred for each other.

Obviously the manifestation of the projection of the opposite sex component onto their partners lies behind this conflict. Just as in alchemy, keeping an even temperature becomes a major problem in most marital and close personal relationships! The outcome is very often an over-heating as exemplified by arguments and over-emotional outbursts, resulting in a drying up of the personal relationship, or alternatively an under-heating shown in passive aggression and withdrawal, leading to a cooling down and a returning to the black confusion so characteristic of marriages in which psychological development has been stagnated or curtailed. More of this will be discussed in the chapters on marriage and anima and animus.

Rubedo

According to the fifteenth-century alchemist Norton, 'red is the last in the work of alchemy'; and, according to Aristotle, 'the philospher's stone [red] is the grand finale of the system – the final cause that can reproduce itself'. In the rubedo phase the alchemist's work comes to an end; he opens the retort and hopefully the philosopher's stone begins to radiate a cosmically healing effect. In psychological terms, with reference to the individuation process, the opposites can be seen as being united or alternatively in precise Jungian terms, a reconciliation of the opposites has occurred, and in so doing the Self is brought into being or consciousness.

In alchemical terms the 'philosopher's gold' has been produced, the stone has been produced, the starting-point and the goal of the opus has been completed and, in Marie-Louise von Franz's terms, one can have that experience of standing on solid ground inside of oneself.

In alchemical language the final stage and indeed the goal is contained in the Latin formula *solve et coagula*, which can be paraphrased as meaning 'out of dissolution unity'. More precisely, according to the French alchemist Piobb, the formula refers to the task of analysing all the elements in yourself, dissolving all that is inferior in you, even though you break in doing so, then with the strength acquired from the preceding operation congeal (that is, crystallise). Thus it becomes clear that alchemy was the necessary historical link for Jung and provided the necessary validation of what I have already stated several times is the essence of Jungian psychology; that is, the reconciliation of opposites within. It is this reconciliation and the binding together of the fixed and volatile principles that produces the stone. That is, the recognition, the acceptance and the integration of opposites leads to their transcendence and the experience of Self – the production of the philosopher's gold, the gold that is not common gold. The pursuit of 'common gold' is the pursuit of literality, and the denial of life as a symbolic process. However, regrettably, contemporary man seems obsessed with literal gold as he avariciously pursues materialism. As James Hillman says 'literalism is sickness. Whenever we are caught in a literal view, a literal belief, a literal statement, we have lost the imaginative metaphorical perspective to ourselves and our world.'*

The denigration of alchemy as mere superstitious nonsense by modern rational thinking represents such a loss, and is symptomatic of the sickness of literality, so pervasive and characteristic of the last two centuries of Western civilisations.

*James Hillman, *Loose Ends*, Spring Publications, 1975, p. 3.

7. Anima and Animus

In the previous chapter, on alchemy, I attempted to elucidate the fundamental theme of alchemy as being the production of the philosopher's gold, the *lapis philosophorum* or the philosopher's stone, all of which I indicated were symbols for Self. Hence the alchemists were not concerned with making common gold, although no doubt, just as there exists literally minded people today, some of them thought that this was what alchemy was about. They did not, as I indicated in the previous chapter, draw any distinction between mind and matter; hence they can be seen as attempting to redeem the spirit (stone) imprisoned in matter and at the same time attempting to redeem the Self, or bringing it into consciousness, from the darkness and primal chaos, the *prima materia* of the unconscious mind. In this production I discussed that there appeared to exist three stages:

1. Nigredo: darkness or blackening.
2. Albedo: whiteness or whitening.
3. Rubedo: redness or colouring of gold.

I outlined that each of these stages could be seen as equivalent or symbolic expressions of the stages of individuation; individuation being that process by which we move towards the integration of opposites, their transcendence, and finally the bringing into consciousness of the Self. That is, these three stages can be seen as three distinct stages in the process of completing our Selves or, if you like, these three stages can be seen as three stages in the redemptive process of recovering our Spirit, Soul or Self from the unconscious. I also outlined that the nigredo phase could be seen as the equivalent or rather parallel to the first stage of individuation; that is, recognition and integration of our shadow aspects, those dark spots in ourselves that have been repressed out of consciousness into the personal unconscious from where they reappear via dreams and/or projections onto others of the same sex.

The second stage, albedo, I discussed as the parallel or equivalent to the integration of opposites; in alchemical terms the conjunction, the *hieros gamos*, the chymical marriage or the *mysterium coniunctionis* – in short the marriage between male and female. It is this stage of alchemy, the middle stage, the albedo, that forms the central theme of the present chapter on anima and animus.

You will recall that the alchemical opus began with the *prima materia*, which usually was composed of lead, tin, copper and iron, which, I suggested, using the astrological symbolism, were symbolic of:

Limitation or Contraction (Saturn – Lead)	vs	Expansion (Jupiter – Tin)
Love (Venus – Copper)	vs	Aggression (Mars – Iron)

Put another way, in terms that are hopefully becoming familiar, the first material can be seen as consisting of opposites, and this is entirely consistent with Jungian theory, which is about the reconciliation of opposites.

Alchemy, of course, being an unconscious projection of the same task, is inevitably about opposites. Indeed, what becomes apparent in studying alchemy and tracing its historical roots is that it has from the earliest beginnings been preoccupied with opposites or, as it was referred to in Chinese alchemy, the principle or doctrine of two contraries, which dates back to approximately the third century BC. In fact one can find the original impetus of the doctrine of two contraries in the Chinese notion of Yin and Yang, which can be dated to the sixth century BC. So, in talking of the opposites or the doctrine of two contraries, it is important to realise that we are *not* discussing anything new.

Indeed, as the nineteenth-century French scholar of alchemy, Hoefer, in his *History of Chemistry*, published in 1866, says in general terms, the systems that confront the intelligence remain basically unchanged throughout the ages, although they assume different forms. He continues by asserting that through mistaking form as basis one concedes an unfavourable opinion of the sequence. In other words, in mistaking the form of an idea for its content, or process, we are apt to undervalue or even dismiss the continuity of the idea. Hoefer concludes by stating that 'there is nothing so disastrous in science as the arrogant dogmatism which despises the past and admires nothing but the present'.* In this spirit I think it is important in discussing the more or less contemporary idea of anima or animus to reflect upon the varying form these ideas have taken over the centuries and carefully note the underlying continuity of their basis.

*F. Hoefer, *Histoire de la Chimie*, Paris, 1866. vol. 1, p. 249.

As I have already said, it was from Richard Wilhelm's translation of *The Secret of the Golden Flower* that Jung received his first solid confirmation of his own ideas. Included in the *Golden Flower* is reference to the two concepts of Soul as personified in Hun and P'o, the male and female aspects of Soul, which directly paralleled Jung's concepts of anima and animus. However, in addition to Hun and P'o, which respectively represent the 'cloud demon' perhaps air and the earthbound 'white ghost', Chinese alchemy as early as the third century included the earlier Chinese or Taoist idea, or principle, of Yin/Yang. In the Taoist tradition the first matter of the universe eventually gave rise to the two principles possessing opposite characters:

Yin = feminine
(negative, heavy and earthy)
Yang = masculine
(positive, light and fiery)

Alternatively Yang is the sky and seen as masculine and the element is fire, whereas Yin is the earth and feminine and the appropriate element is water. The Chinese alchemists held the view that by interaction the two contraries gave rise to the five elements composing or constituting the material world; that is, water, fire, wood, gold and earth.

However, what one finds is a constant repetition of these two principles throughout time, just as Hoefer suggests that the form only changes, the basis remaining immutable. So we find, for example, in ancient India, the Hindus held that metals were born of the union of Hara (Shiva) and Parvati (consort of Hara), through the help of Agni, the god of fire. In this mythology Mercury (water or *aqua permanens*) was associated with the semen of Hara, sulphur with Agni and the earth with Parvati. In Egyptian mythology one finds the sun god, Osiris, regarded as the active principle, vivifying influence or originating source of energy and power, and Isis the moon goddess as the passive and receptive god. In fact the sun and the moon or, as the alchemists would call them, sol and lunar (sometimes depicted as rex/regina), were often used as expressions of the active principle (the sun) and the passive female principle (the moon). As with Osiris and Isis, the principles of the sun and the moon were held to give rise to all things by their conjunction or interaction. Indeed, I think one can suggest with some plausibility that the Catholic tradition of the virgin birth may well be one additional contemporary representation of the interaction of these two principles giving birth. For example, the female or passive principle can be seen as Mary, the active or male principle the fire, as the Holy Spirit and the product of these interactions as Christ or Self. In specific chemical terms of alchemy one comes across the constant reference to mercury and sulphur, which were seen by Jabir (Islamic eighth-century alchemist) as being exhalations from the interior of the earth (which links it directly back to the Chinese views of the origin of Yin/Yang), and that by combining in different proportions and in different degrees of purity giving rise to various metals and minerals (which also links it to the Chinese concept of the derivation of the five elements).

In European alchemy it seems that sulphur and mercury were the two substances most commonly used in conjunction with the basic material or *prima materia* of lead, tin, copper and iron. Here again then we see the two contraries, since one can take the symbolic view that sulphur is equivalent or symbolic of the spirit or fire because of its combustability, and mercury is the symbolic equivalent of the spirit of liquidity (water). Thus from the interaction of sulphur (fire) and mercury (water) we get gold; that is, the marriage of the opposites – namely sulphur and mercury or fire and water – leads to the chymical marriage or the production of the philosopher's gold or Self.

Paracelsus, the sixteenth-century alchemist, added an additional ingredient to this, namely salt, which can be seen as the symbolic equivalent of body in which the conjunction is contained, and we will see how this relates to the contemporary issue of marriage. Not only, then, can we trace this continuing theme of opposites or two contraries through from ancient Chinese thought to mediaeval European alchemy, we can trace it also right up to the twentieth century in modern physics and the conceptualisation of the atomic structure of electrons and protons. What are electrons and protons other than negatively and positively charged particles?, the mercury and sulphur of alchemy, the Yin and Yang of Chinese thought. In this physical dimension, given that I suspect the distinction between mind and matter introduced to Western man by Descartes is artificial, and its perpetuation is a reflection of the inflationary effects of rational thinking as a superior function, it ought to come as no surprise when I state that the psychological dimension of electrons and protons, or mercury and sulphur, or Yin and Yang, can (I believe) be seen in Jung's concepts of anima and animus, the male and female aspects of the psyche. It is also important to point out that just as the marriage between mercury and sulphur leads to, or assists in, the production of this philosopher's stone, or alternatively the interaction between Yin and Yang gives rise to the material conditions of the world. So also can one argue that the marriage between anima and animus in the joining or conjunction of the opposite sexual elements within us leads to the emergence, production or liberation of our own philosopher's stone from the imprisonment in the darkness of the unconscious mind. In other words, behind the bond of the contrasexual elements in our psyche lies the Self. From the work done in the albedo phase, in the whitening, comes the rubedo stage and the production of the philospher's gold or stone.

ANIMA AND ANIMUS

Having laid the groundwork for the universality of the two contraries, let me now turn in more detail to the personal realm of these two principles, which we have seen in one form or another throughout time. In reading Jung on the anima and the animus, it becomes readily apparent that he talks of and discussed the anima, that is the feminine aspects of men, in far more detail than he discusses the animus, the masculine aspects of women. No doubt a fairly straightforward explanation for this is simply that Jung was male and had direct personal experience and familiarity with the anima. Likewise, after some initial hesitancy on my part, I have decided to proceed by discussing the anima first, since I am more familiar with it. Furthermore, I think that given the enormous social change that has occurred in relation to women, consideration of the animus is necessarily more complex than consideration of the anima. Before proceeding specifically to the anima, I think there are a few general points one can make, which are applicable to both aspects and indeed hopefully contribute to an understanding of both.

In the first place, both anima and animus are derived from two roots or sources. At the most basic and powerful level they are archetypal forces and belong to that level of mind called the collective unconscious or, as it appears to be increasingly referred to in contemporary Jungian circles, the objective psyche (to distinguish it from the personal unconscious). In volume 17 of his *Collected Works (Development of Personality)* Jung provides a definition of the anima that encompasses this archetypal quality, this inherited quality that comes as part of being a human being and not as a product of being a particular human being:

> Every man carried within him the eternal image of woman, not the image of this or that particular woman but a definitive feminine image. This image is fundamentally unconscious, an hereditary factor of primordial origin engraved in the living organic system of the man, an imprint or 'archetype' of all the ancestral experiences of the female, a deposit, as it were, of all the impressions ever made by woman. (*CW* 17:198)

I think it fair to state that at the collective unconscious level one can simply substitute the word woman or female where appropriate for the terms man or male, and the same definition suffices for the animus at the collective unconscious level of women. Because at this level it is an archetype, the whole dilemma of whether archetypes have a biological basis or not once again emerges. If, as I have discussed earlier, archetypes are innate behavioural patterns that have resulted from the endless repetition of specific experiences of human beings throughout time, then it seems to me highly probable that the anima and animus are mental representations or archetypal images of the minority of female genes in a man's body on the one hand, and the minority of male genes in a female's body on the other hand. Just as the body itself exhibits representations of the opposite genetic structure, so also would it seem reasonable to argue that the collective unconscious level, the anima and animus, are psychic or mental representations of the minority gene structure within each human being. Jung himself states exactly this when he says:

The anima is presumably a psychic representation of the minority of female genes in a man's body. This is all the more probable since the same figure is not to be found in the imagery of a woman's unconscious. There is a corresponding figure, however, that plays an equivalent role, yet it is not a woman's image but a man's. This masculine figure in a woman's psychology has been termed animus.* (*CW* 11:30)

Thus in simple terms one can say that every man has a collected image of a woman in his unconscious mind, the effect of which is to help him to apprehend the nature of a woman. This image, as I have just quoted, is an archetype, a mental representation of the age-old experience of man with woman and, in the case of the animus, woman with man. It is perhaps important to point out at this stage that I believe that not only does anima help a man to apprehend the nature of a woman on the outside, but the anima also helps a man to apprehend the nature of a woman within himself: the reverse holding true for females.

PERSONAL LEVEL OF THE ANIMA AND ANIMUS

In addition to the archetypal nature of the anima and animus there also exists a personal unconscious level of these archetypes, which is basically determined and affected by a man's or woman's personal experience of the opposite sex, the respective experience that comes through contact with the opposite sex. In fact, Jung asserts that (consistent with all archetypes) it is through projection that we first became aware of their existence, so men and women find that they become conscious of this image, of the archetypal image, only through an actual contact with an individual of the opposite sex. Then the image is projected onto that person, and in the case of a man the first and most important personal experience of a woman that occurs in his life and becomes a focus for this projection is his mother. For a woman it is quite obviously the father. Given normal development, the image is then projected onto various men or women who attract individuals. Unfortunately, the image that is projected does not always match too well, and a time soon comes in which an awareness of the mis-match arrives, the perception of this mis-match is the cause of many a disturbance in marriages and/or love affairs.

The third factor that the anima and animus have in common is their relationship to the persona, which is essentially a compensatory relationship. The persona, as we have already discussed, has the function of relating the psyche to the outside world. The anima and animus have the equivalent function of relating the ego or consciousness to the inner world. In this sense, then, the anima and animus both act as mediators between the conscious and unconscious mind, where they then become personified in fantasies, dreams or visions; they represent an opportunity to understand something that has previously been unconscious.

Often what one finds is that the anima and animus have a direct compensatory relationship with the persona so that, for example, the very powerful and masculine businessman who identifies with his persona is often inwardly victimised by irrational moods, depressions, compulsive sexual fantasies, etc., etc. Likewise, the female who identifies with an overly feminine, all-to-sweet female persona is often unconsciously preoccupied with power, exceedingly demanding and determined to have her own way. This is simply because the face the psyche shows to the outside world has its opposite face shown to the inner world and is reflected in the anima or animus.

A fourth factor that both anima and animus have in common is that they both have a negative and positive aspect or face. That is, anima or animus is not all good as some people are inclined to believe. Both aspects of the psyche can be extremely destructive, some manifestations of which we will discuss when discussing the two separately.

ANIMA

Having discussed what they have in common, let me now turn to each of these aspects of the psyche and discuss them separately as they play out their life in the individual psyches of men and women. Jung once said that anima produces moods and the animus opinions. One can further add that the interaction between anima and animus produces animosity! By moods, Jung was referring to the negative aspect of the anima, which is the first form in which men meet or come across this aspect of themselves. For men in Western society traditionally defined feminine traits – such as feeling, compassion and intuition – very often get severely repressed in the interest of the masculine ego-consciousness, and thus are deeply buried in the personal unconscious, where often they are only to reappear in the form of projection onto women on the outside of men. Hence some of the vitriolic verbal attacks that husbands or men make on their wives or feminine companions have behind them what has sometimes been called the activity of lady anima. That is, a man projects all his negative feeling about himself and the feminine parts of himself onto the woman on the outside, when in fact it is the woman within his own under-developed feminine side that he is really having the argument with. Not infrequently the anima will appear or manifest itself in erotic fantasies and/or sexual deviations. This is because by and large the governing principle of the anima or the feminine aspect of a man's psyche is eros – the principle of relationships, nurturance and relatedness. However, eros is in my view best conceptualised as a continuum, like a spectrum of light. At one end is sexuality in its most primitive and least developed form – pornography, since here the relationship is one of non-involvement, simply looking at. In the middle of this continuum of eros or spectrum of eros is normal sexual relationships, including erotic fantasies. At the upper end of eros is spiritual growth and development. Tantric yoga is a classic example of this intertwining of sexuality and spiritual growth.

Thus as eros is the governing principle of the anima or the Soul, since anima translates as Soul or inner personality, its first emergence into consciousness in addition to its negative form of moodiness is very often in the form of erotic sexual fantasy. This is simply because men have so repressed their feminine side that it is as equally under-developed and immature as the persona is over-developed and over-matured. Remembering that the anima exists in a compensatory or balancing relationship to the persona to the extent that a man has developed his outer image, his inner image or Soul or anima would, to that extent, be under-developed. Thus it is not unusual for its first emergence to be in the less mature form of an interest in pornography or erotic fantasy. As a rule of thumb, what we yearn for sexually, whether it be in the fantasy or otherwise, is usually a symbolic representation of what we need in order to become whole. Hence the erotic fantasies that men experience when the anima makes her presence felt in the man's consciousness have to be understood symbolically. Very often they mean that a man needs to form a relationship with the feminine part of himself and all that is contained therein. Images of women therefore appearing in a man's sexual fantasies become representations to him of his other missing half, the other side of his personality, the side to which he needs to relate.

In fact the key word is 'relate', since it is in forming

a conscious relationship with his feminine aspects, or anima, that the negative side of moodiness tends to disappear or at least be integrated. It is when we deny figures in the unconscious, reject or ignore the anima, that it – or for that matter the animus – turns against us and shows its negative face. When the anima or animus is accepted, understood and a relationship begun to be built with it, then it is the positive side that tends to appear and be available for conscious awareness. However, to perceive first of all this side of himself requires considerable conscious effort on a man's part and this is perhaps why Jung referred to the encounter with the anima or animus as the 'masterpiece' of individuation.

In the first place, it requires a man to overcome the very marked and pronounced tendency to think of himself as exclusively masculine or in the case of a woman to think of herself as exclusively feminine. In our rather young and, I feel, psychologically undeveloped culture, we tend to adhere fairly tightly it seems to me to stereotypes, despite the emergence of women's liberation. Therefore it is very difficult for the average individual person to shift his or her perception of himself or herself from the biological gender of either exclusively male or female. It also requires a second challenge, or hurdle to overcome, and that is that our conscious life simply rests on a sea, a vast sea, of an inner world of which we know very little. Again in this vast space of ours that we call Australia, I fear that we not infrequently suffer from sunburnt psyches in so far as we are aware only of our outside or ego consciousness and not the vast sea of unconsciousness upon which the outside rests.

In general I believe Australians treat or regard their inner worlds not as something objective and real, but ironically as 'that's just your imagination'. The external world reigns supreme and the inner world is often relegated to the unreal. Given these barriers or hurdles to overcome in a man's psyche, if he is to build any sort of relationship with his anima, that personification of the inner world or Soul, then it is not surprising that men in general resort to projecting this part of themselves on the outside and forming a relationship with the female on the outside of themselves rather than recognising it as also being part of themselves within. Herein lies the cause of many extra-marital relationships, the seemingly inexplicable case of the ever-so-respectable professor or lawyer leaving his family and going off to live with a young, sexually attractive woman who seemingly is the antithesis of the type of person he will be attracted to. Herman Hesse's novel *Steppenwolf* describes such a character, who in his isolation from his own feminine side is seduced by a quite ordinary young woman. However, the outcome of the relationship in this novel, unlike the usual outcome in life itself, is to initiate the man into a confrontation with himself.

What I have often seen in my everyday practice is that the man goes on believing that the woman he has fallen in love with is actually all of those things that he sees in her, and he refuses to recognise and accept the projection. In this refusal he refuses to realise that the object of his passion is actually part of himself. I think the explanation for this lies in part in the fact that the feminine traits of men are so severely repressed from consciousness that the anima is usually equivalent to an adolescent age if not younger. In line with Jungian thought, the anima is seen as usually having four distinct stages of psychological development. Another way of thinking about this is that the feminine aspect of man has four clearly defined developmental stages and the more severely the anima is repressed, then the more powerful will be the earlier stages when it first reappears. These four stages consist of:

1. A sexual/physical anima, for example, Bo Derek, or, more traditionally, Marilyn Monroe.
2. A sexual/emotional type of female, for example, classically Helen of Troy.
3. The emotional, spiritually mediumistic type of female, the example from literature of such a figure will be in Rider Haggard's novel *She*.
4. The purely spiritual woman who is often symbolised by wisdom transcending even the most holy and pure. A classic example of this would be Shulamite in the Song of Solomon and in art the Mona Lisa comes nearest to such a wisdom anima. The Greek goddess of wisdom, Athena, is an example from mythology.

The level of a man's anima development will be reflected in the types of projections he makes upon women in the outside world and the types of relationships with women that he forms. The level of this development will largely depend on the extent to which a man's ego-consciousness is identified with his persona. That is, to what extent he has developed only his outward masculine traits and ignored his inner world. The levels of anima development also quite clearly reflect the increasing level of development of the eros principle within him. If a man can come to realise that his moods, irrational attractions or repulsions to certain women, his seemingly inexplicable erotic fantasies are all part of himself, then the anima tends to reveal as a consequence of this awareness her positive side and then acts as a guide to the inner world. In this capacity, as mediator, she helps in building a relationship to the unconscious mind and thereby aids in the development and emergence of Self. As Marie-Louise von Franz says in an essay on individuation:

> Only the painful (but essentially simple) decision to take one's fantasies and feelings seriously can at this stage prevent a complete stagnation of the inner process of individuation, because only in this way can a man discover what this figure means as an inner reality.*

Because most males in Western society tend to develop as their superior function thinking, with sensation as the auxiliary, their soul image, or anima, tends to join up with the repressed or inferior function. Hence the anima tends to be a primitive, romantic emotional embodiment or personification of the feeling and intuitive functions. Thus, because men have not developed the so-called feminine traits, the anima in males tends to be predictable and to follow a predictable pattern of development or stagnation. This begins, as a rule, with the evocation of sexual fantasies or sexual acting out, and then moves through, if the development is not arrested, to the spiritual aspects of anima. However, here often they can be

*'The Process of Individuation' in C. G. Jung et al., *Man and his Symbols*, Doubleday/Alders Books, 1964, p. 188.

waylaid by the occult or other guru-type figures, who provide suitable objects or persons to carry anima projections and once again prevent the conscious awareness of these aspects.

ANIMUS

However, it seems to me that the situation is vastly different with the animus, the so-called masculine part of women's psyche. I think it is vastly different largely because of the social changes that have occurred in the past fifteen to twenty years exemplified by the women's movement and that such changes have fundamentally brought about a change in female consciousness. Thus, where the man's feminine part and development tends to be predictable, this is not the case, as far as I can ascertain, with the animus aspect of women. However, within the Jungian framework, the animus, like the anima, is considered at least theoretically to have four clearly defined stages of development from the most primitive through to the most spiritual, depending on the woman's inner development of those aspects of herself. These four stages of development, paralleling the anima, are:

1. *Physical.* Here the emphasis in the animus is on physical power. Modern-day sporting heroes, such as football players, or fictional characters, such as Tarzan, would seem to be personifications of a physical animus.
2. *Man of Deeds.* Here the emphasis is on the hunter, the adventurer type. A recent example of such a Man of Deeds would be such a character as Sir Edmund Hillary, or modern-day astronauts.

3. *Man of Word.* Here one tends to find political and intellectual figures, where the power is derived from the power of the world. A contemporary example would appear to be, in Australia at least, Bob Hawke.
4. *Man of Meaning.* Here the emphasis is derived from the spiritual quality of the man and the spiritual guiding quality. A classic example would be Mahatma Gandhi and indeed Christ.

Where the governing principle of anima was eros, the governing principle of animus is logos. That is, the power of meaning and competence is derived from tasks, whether they be physical, intellectual, emotional or spiritual. Thus, for women traditionally, the animus has been to do with the outside world and establishing competence and meaning in the context of the outer world, whereas the anima has traditionally for men been to do with establishing a relationship with the inner world. However, the changing social structure has, I think, given rise to the situation, ironically perhaps, where for many women the animus is actually well developed and the task is to develop the anima, develop a relationship with their inner world, when they have spent the first half of their lives developing competence in the outer world, usually in the form of a career. For such women, perhaps somewhat paradoxically, the emergence of mid-life involves more anima-like issues, such as a conflict over whether they will have a baby or not; that is, develop the feeling function. However, for the moment, to return to the traditional Jungian arguments concerning animus, Emma Jung (Jung's wife), who has written an excellent book on an anima and animus, states as follows:

What we women have to overcome in our relation to the animus is not pride but lack of self confidence and the resistance of inertia. For us, it is not as though we had to demean ourselves, but as if we had to lift ourselves.*

This quotation from Emma Jung anticipates by some forty years the effects of the women's movement in Australia. Traditionally, the animus has been associated or seen as an embodiment of a woman's inferior function, and these traditionally have been seen as being composed of thinking and sensation, those functions in which logos and not eros is the governing principle. However, as just mentioned, nowadays, with the breakdown of the stereotype role prescription for women, increasingly what one sees is the animus is well-developed and the struggle is to develop the anima face of the psyche, sometimes personified in dilemma of whether one conceives a child or not.

Symbolically such as issue can be seen as the need for growth. Hence in some ways one can see both anima and animus as increasingly being about building a relationship with the inferior functions that have been repressed out of consciousness in the interest of developing the superior functions in the first half of life. The effect of the women's movement and social change has been that women now are freer to choose which aspect they develop first, animus or anima. This freedom is remote for men, who are still directed by stereotyped expectations, which result in the feminine or anima aspects being rejected in the first half of life thereby condemning them to immaturity.

*Emma Jung, *Animus and Anima,* Spring Publications, 1978, p. 23.

8. Marriage

As I have already indicated, this chapter on marriage can be best regarded as the third in a trilogy that connects alchemy, anima and animus, with contemporary marriage. Undoubtedly the underlying theme of this trilogy is that of the recognition and reconciliation of opposites, and further that this theme finds its perhaps most dramatic expression in the work of the alchemists, since they can be regarded as projecting this task onto or into matter. Hence, in a somewhat ironical manner, the alchemists provide us at the same time with the most objective description of this underlying process that connects this trilogy.

In the chapter on alchemy I attempted to elucidate that alchemy had both an exoteric and esoteric face, or if you prefer an outer face pointing to the outside world and an inner face pertaining to the inside or inner world. I attempted to state in passing that, from the sixteenth century on, the exoteric or extroverted tradition of alchemy had dominated, culminating in the twentieth-century obsession with rational thinking, empirical science and in an almost childish belief in facts and a childish obsession with proof. The essence of this so-called scientific viewpoint, which finds its major protagonist in Descartes and the split between mind and matter, or observer and observed, is the idea of causality. The existing scientific paradigm or model that we have inherited and hold in our psyche is the model of linear causality (that is, if something happens it must have had a cause!) and if no reason can be discovered then most people will simply conclude that we do not yet know *the* cause. Hence a wealth of psychic phenomena (for example, parapsychological phenomena) is simply ignored by much of the scientific community and mankind in general and denigrated as superstitious nonsense simply because we cannot discern the cause and fit such phenomena into our linear causal model. Now this is not to say that certain psychological phenomena are without causes, since obviously the cause can be demonstrated, but the problem arises when we believe (religiously!) that *all* phenomena must conform to our ego-conscious view of linear causality.

Jung developed the idea of synchronicity as an additional model or alternative model or explanation for certain phenomenon, such as the I Ching. Indeed he called one of his papers, published in 1952, 'Synchronicity: an acausal principle'.* Synchronicity simply means that some things co-occur, so-called coincidentally and not in a linear causal fashion. So, although science as we know it, the extroverted face of alchemy, the face that has focused on nature or the outside world, has progressed enormously, all models of the world have limitations, and these tend to show up when the model of the world, in this case the logical positivist model or scientific model, comes across seemingly inexplicable phenomena.

However, human beings seem remarkably maladaptive at times, and instead of struggling often to form a new hypothesis to explain previously inexplicable phenomena, what most scientists and indeed people in general do is to cling even more tenaciously

*In *CW*, vol. 9, part 1.

to the old views. Universities can be seen as institutionalised versions of old views, and indeed being an academic has, I suspect, very often functioned as a barrier to creativity, since any new idea is attacked, whether in a thesis or professional paper, usually on the grounds that it has not conformed to the requirements of the prevailing scientific method. The scientific method has – perhaps not unexpectedly, given the nature of opposites within the psyche – become the scientists' religion! There is indeed a touch of irony about this, since the very same scientists would claim that logical thinking and science is overcoming simplistic religious beliefs in man. The irony no doubt is that he religiously goes about proving this!

All of this is a roundabout way of saying that the exoteric face of alchemy, reflective of the rise of thinking as the superior function, has culminated in our highly technological society and led to a relative loss of the esoteric or inner face of alchemy. Now if for a moment you can hold the idea of a parallel relationship between alchemy and marriage, then I think some interesting issues can emerge. The direct parallel is that alchemy, as we have seen, is a symbolically expressive act of the process of individuation. The process, you recall, is the one of moving towards completing our Selves. Indeed, within this context we have seen that the second stage of alchemy was concerned with what was called the chymical marriage, the *hieros gamos,* or the mystical marriage of opposites, and that this stage was called the albedo phase or the middle phase. On a psychological-alchemical level, this was seen as the marriage between mercury and sulphur; on the inner psychological plane as a marriage between the male (animus) and female (anima) aspects of an individual's psyche.

Now, just as we have split off the esoteric aspects of alchemy and produced this obsession with the outside aspects in the form of scientific chemistry, so also I believe have we done exactly the same thing with marriage. This ought not be too surprising since the second stage of alchemy, the albedo phase, can be seen as a direct parallel to contemporary marriage, where once again man is attempting to marry the opposite, that is male and female. However, he, like the chemists, has committed the extroverted mistake of imagining, indeed believing, that the outside marriage is the only marriage; that the legal, institutionalised marriage in the external world or exoteric form as we know it, is the only marriage; that mercury and sulphur is all we are about. In short, we have also lost the esoteric view of marriage, we have lost the inner view, the fact that marriage is not only about being married to someone of the opposite sex on the *outside* of ourselves (the chemical or scientific marriage), it is at the same time about being married to the *inside* of ourselves, the alchemical or esoteric marriage, the albedo stage of the work.

Marriage, then, in this context also has two faces and represents the contemporary alchemical opus. But we, like the ancient alchemists, have projected the inside work onto the outside and have failed to see the inner or esoteric face of marriage. Another way of stating this, perhaps a clearer way, is that in every marriage there is both a conscious marriage and an unconscious marriage. The unconscious marriage is personified – and I stress personified, not entirely described – by the Jungian concepts of anima and animus, that is the marriage, or as it so often happens the non-marriage, between the unconscious feminine side of a man and the unconscious masculine side of a woman with their own conscious Self.

As we shall come to see, it is this inner courtship that brings about the manifestation or conscious difficulties between marriage partners. If marital problems were simply at the level of the conscious marriage, the outside or extrovert or exoteric marriage, then I believe information would cure them. The reality is that marital difficulties persist in spite of and despite the most honourable conscious intention of the marriage partners themselves. It is the unconscious esoteric marriage that causes conflict and ultimately brings about divorce. It seems to me that in this last half of the present century we are dominated by technological and extroverted views and therefore project the inner face onto the outer world and perpetuate the mistake of science in assuming that only the outside marriage is the real marriage.

A major verification of this technological view of marriage, of this extroverted view of marriage, can be seen in the utterly amazing proliferation of how-to-do-it marriage and sex manuals that pervade our bookstores these days. There has developed a literal mountain of such literature, and indeed in the United States of America there exists a prolific number of university departments exclusively dedicated to marriage and sexual studies and counsellor training. That such a proliferation should find its initial and most powerful impetus and source in the USA ought not be surprising, since my impression is that as a culture and society it is an extroverted one, and thereby has a magnificent obsession with the outside world, resulting in its technological sophistication. The tragedy, it seems to me, is that that technological view, that exoteric view, pervades their entire lives, hence marriage, sex and personal relationships are approached and perceived as simply yet another technological problem. Almost without exception, the plethora of marriage manuals and such equivalent books originate from the USA – such is man's insatiable desire for vulgar gold! Such also is his naïve and religious belief in the power of rational information! Such is the level of nonsense it seems to me that the extroverted and exoteric view in being pursued to its limits produces! Behind all this technology, behind all this information, is in my opinion the childish hope that one can acquire the solutions to life without the pain of understanding. As Jung once stated in his only written work on marriage: 'There is no birth of consciousness without pain.'*

The pursuit of technology in any area, but specifically in the realm of personal relationships, reflects the literality of those alchemists who sought the vulgar gold, and thought that by making vulgar gold they would become rich, and who thereby miss the point of the process itself. It is perhaps no accident, and one might say that it is highly significant, that a proliferation of technology, an over-accentuation of the outer view, the exoteric view, finds its major expression within the context of a highly capitalistic society in which the acquisition of wealth (vulgar gold) is the

* *The Development of Personality*, volume 17 of *CW*, p. 193.

raison d'être. I fear that we in Australia are moving precariously close to the same fate. This preoccupation with the technology of marriage, with the chemistry of marriage, rather than the alchemistry of marriage, has also contributed in my view to the prevalence and indeed perpetuation of the fantasy that the end-product and purpose of marriage is freedom from conflict and ultimate happiness. The Jungian and, indeed, any psychoanalytic view, as we shall come to discuss, holds a very contrary view of marriage to that of the happiness myth. Again such a myth is closely akin to the motivation and hopes of the literally and concretely minded alchemists, who pursued their freedom from conflict and happiness in the pursuit of ordinary gold (that is, outer gold rather than inner gold).

JUNG'S VIEWS ON MARRIAGE

To return to the point I made a little earlier, I would now like to pursue the description of marriage consisting of both a conscious and unconscious marriage and use this idea as the appropriate point to introduce Jung's view of marriage. Following this, I would then like to go on to discuss briefly one of the contemporary Jungian theories of marriage, and then finally return to exploring the purpose of marriage, drawing upon the alchemical notion and idea of redemption and salvation as opposed to happiness.

It never ceases to amaze me that in eighteen immense volumes of writing Jung managed to write only twelve pages specifically on marriage. These twelve pages, entitled 'Marriage as a Psychological Relationship', were written in 1931, and are contained in volume 17 of his *Collected Works,* pages 189-201. This, in large part, reflects the fact that Jung's psychology is concerned fundamentally with the individual's psyche and not his or her relationship with the outside world. Its focus is on the relationships within the inner world as seen in the personification of archetypes; for example, anima and animus. This in turn, I feel, very much reflects the personality of Jung himself, which we have discussed earlier in this book: the quiet, withdrawn and somewhat lonely person that he appears to have been. Personally, I think it a great pity that he did not write more on marriage, and that he did not either find time or have the inclination to expand his immense knowledge of alchemy and apply it to contemporary marriage. One is left wondering what it says of his own marriage, and indeed some writers have noted the significant omission of references to his wife in, for example, his autobiography, *Memories, Dreams and Reflections.* I suspect that this can be explained in part by the fact that Jung was fundamentally occupied with exploring his own internal marriage, and it was this that he felt was important and had to be written about.

With respect to what Jung has written on marriage, two essential ideas or concepts stand out. One is reflected in the title of the paper on marriage; that it is a psychological relationship. The other basic idea, one that has gained considerable prominence in contemporary Jungian thinking on marriage and relationships, is the concept of what has been termed the 'contained' and 'container'. Firstly, to the idea of marriage as a psychological relationship. On the surface this may appear a self-evident statement; however, Jung had a very precise notion of what a psychological relationship was. For him there was *no* possibility of a psychological relationship unless there was consciousness, and, further, in order to become conscious of oneself, Jung maintained that we must be able to distinguish ourselves from others. So consciousness in this context has something to do with being separate and yet attached; a theme that has re-emerged in contemporary Jungian theory on marriage, as we shall see later. Unless there is a degree of separateness it is impossible, it seems, to develop a sense of oneself different and distinguishable from one's partner or others. Hence an optimal level of separateness in a marriage would be in Jung's terms a necessary precondition for consciousness. Thus, for Jung:

> Whenever we speak of a 'psychological relationship' we presuppose one that is conscious, for there is no such thing as a psychological relationship between two people when one is in a state of unconsciousness. (*CW* 17:189)

In other words, what Jung is asserting, it seems to me, is that the possibility of a relationship (that is, a psychological relationship) is limited by the degree to which each partner is conscious of who they are as individuals. He argues that people can have a physical relationship, but without a sufficient level of consciousness the relationship is without choice, since people merely act from unconscious motives and their connections to each other is via projection, not a conscious relationship. In other words, where people are unconscious of themselves and their motives, they place all these unconscious aspects of themselves onto the partner in the relationship or the marriage, and hence this so-called relationship is not to the person as a separate individual, but merely as an object, or container, of what is unconsciously within oneself. In short, it is a relationship with one's own unconscious in the projected form, and to that extent Jung would declare that it was not a psychological relationship because it was without ego-consciousness, without a distinction between Self and other.

Jung held the view, one that has been consistently substantiated in psychotherapeutic practice, that the choice of one's mate is fundamentally unconscious, because the age at which the average young person gets married he or she possesses only a limited amount of consciousness, only a partially developed sense of identity. Therefore Jung concludes that it is the strength of the bond to the parents that unconsciously influences the choice of husband or wife, either positively or negatively.

For Jung, one of the major factors that affects mate choice (that is, choice of partner) is the unconscious tie to one's parents. By unconscious tie, what Jung meant was simply 'that children are driven unconsciously in a direction that is intended to compensate for everything that was left unfulfilled in the lives of the parents' (*CW* 17:191). Hence Jung gives the classic example of the excessively moral parents who produce what are called 'immoral' children, or alternatively the irresponsible father who has a son who is consumed by a morbid amount of righteous ambition.

Jung held the view that the choice of partner can and indeed often does reflect these unconscious ties. So, for example, the son who has unconsciously been tied to the mother as a sort of substitute husband for her because the mother's marriage itself lacks feeling or emotional attachment, might marry a woman whom he perceives as inferior to his mother, thereby maintaining the unconscious tie and avoiding the competition. Alternatively, if the tie is a negative one, and he has resented the mother's unconscious attachment to him, he may marry a very domineering, tyrannical woman whom he then slowly but systematically resists and antagonises, as a substitute for the control he felt he never could exercise over his mother.

Jung felt that as most marriages had unconscious choices as their foundation, that most marriages remained primitive and decidedly impersonal, since they merely reflected traditional customs and marital roles. I have called these marriages 'outside marriages' or stereotype marriages, in which very little individualistic development has occurred. Sadly, such marriages are characterised by their impersonal nature and lack of personal conversation. That is not to say that they are not stable; often they are very stable, which is ironically their weakness. The partners involved have opted for a non-struggling relationship, rather than one in which growth, but necessarily conflict, will be present. Jung shows his pessimism when discussing this issue when he says: 'Any mental effort, like the conscious process itself, is so much strain for the ordinary man that he invariably prefers the simple, even when it does not happen to be the truth' (*CW* 17:195). Further on, in relation to conflict and crises, Jung has this to say: 'Seldom or never does a marriage develop into an individual relationship smoothly and without crises' (*CW* 17:193).

The development into an individual relationship is

the transition between a solely ego-based marriage to an awakening of the latent, but powerful, unconscious marriage within each of the partners. This is equivalent to the marriage shifting from a horizontal marriage to the additional quality of also being a vertical marriage. This awakening of the unconscious marriage, the vertical marriage, begins traditionally at the mid-life period. In my experience, one can only realistically expect the ego-based marriage, the horizontal marriage, the extroverted marriage, the one in which the unconscious motives and forces lie dormant, to last about ten to twelve years. Around this time and for then a period of some five to ten years, perhaps, most if not all marriages undergo a transitional crisis as the inner strivings to shift from a stereotype role-directed marriage, persona marriage, to an individualistic or psychological relationship begin to occur.

As I have already said, this stirring in the unconscious mind coincides with the mid-life period in the individual, although by no means, and in fact rarely, does each of the partners begin this process or end it at the same time. By and large the more complex of the two will experience the internal discontent more acutely, and therefore be the first into the mid-life development transitional period. A crisis in a marriage of ten to twelve years' duration usually coincides with the onset of an individual's mid-life crisis, since mid-life is the beginning of a period of enormous psychological change, in which archetypal forces aimed at redressing the imbalance of the consciously developed attitudes are unleashed. This unleashing process is typified in the emergence of anima or animus, and in my terms is the beginning of the true alchemical opus of developing the esoteric marriage or, in Jung's terms, the psychological relationship. Jung, in speaking of the mid-life period, has some powerful and clear words to say:

Middle life is the moment of greatest unfolding, when a man still gives himself to his work with his whole strength and his whole will. But in this very moment evening is born and the second half of life begins. Passion now changes her face and is called duty. 'I want' becomes 'I must' and the turnings of the pathway that once bought surprise and discovery becomes dulled by custom. The wine has fermented and begins to settle and clear. Conservative tendencies develop if all goes well; instead of looking forward one looks backward, most of the time involuntarily and one begins to take stock, to see how one's life has developed up to this point. The real motivations are sought and real discoveries are made. The critical survey of himself and his fate enables a man to recognise his peculiarities. But these insights do not come to him easily; they are gained only through the severest shocks. (*CW* 17:193)

This disunity and discontent, this severest of shocks that individuals feel in mid-life have their source in the unconscious mind, and therefore individuals are often unaware of the real state of things, and as a result they project their discontent onto their partner.

Up until this time, that is this ten- to twelve-year period, the marriage usually has been governed by a process that Jung describes as the 'contained' and the 'container'. In the simplest possible terms it was

Jung's view that a woman was contained spiritually (and we can take that to be the logos principle, thinking spirit) in her husband, and the husband was contained emotionally in his wife. That is to say that Jung was attempting to establish the point that the parts of a woman's psyche that were not in consciousness were projected onto her husband or male partner and literally carried by, or contained by, him. Conversely, according to Jung, a man who could not consciously accept or integrate into consciousness his feminine side will project this side onto his wife or female partner, and she then would literally carry, or contain it, for him. Hence large parts, large slices, of each partner were virtually seen as belonging to or residing in the other; that is, contained by the other. Within the context of 1930, when Jung wrote this article, the sexual roles were stereotyped and rigid, and thus one's partner contained the unconscious opposite aspects of oneself. In the 1930s this unconscious opposite was perhaps best seen as the feminine part of a man and the masculine part of a woman. So what Jung observed in marriage was a woman projecting her animus onto her husband and he, in turn, projecting his anima onto his wife.

Whilst I think this is still valid today, the contemporary view tends to be a broader one, in so far as not only are the anima and animus contained by the partner, but so also are other split-off and lost aspects of the personality that have been repressed from consciousness. What sets the conflict in motion in a marriage, despite how stable and satisfying it has been, is often the erupting into consciousness of this opposite sex or anima/animus component in our psyche. The result of this is that couples start to quarrel incessantly; a man complains bitterly about his wife's moods, the ease of her life, her illogicality, her non-caring, her feminine intuition, etc., etc. In short, a whole list of negative qualities that belong to the woman within him, his anima.

As we have discussed previously, the first form in which a man meets his anima, his feminine side, is usually in the negative form, and usually by projecting this onto the female with which he has a permanent relationship. Likewise a woman will first encounter her animus in the negative form, and project this onto her husband. Thus she will accuse him of being unfeeling, over-rational, thinking only of himself, having no feelings, of being over-critical and perfectionistic, expecting others to live up to his standards, of being opinionated, domineering, etc., etc. – all the qualities that belong to the masculine side in its immature form within her. When this type of accusation starts in earnest after ten or twelve years of marriage, then one can rest assured that mid-life is in full sail and that the internal unconscious marriage is starting to emerge, having been held in check by convention and sterotyped ideas of marriage. The chance or opportunity to begin the task of creating a vertical marriage, a marriage between the opposites within, of developing the psychological relationship that Jung talks of, has arrived. This regretfully is an opportunity that many people turn their backs on. They commit psychological suicide, opt for the death of convention, and wonder why they are bored stiff with each other. Usually we turn our back on the challenge because we are unwilling to work through conflict and perceive the creative seeds that lie within conflict. This is primarily because our consciously limited view of marriage is that it is about happiness, and thus we automatically equate conflict with unhappiness and want to close the conflict off, push it under, or walk away from it by getting a divorce. It seems to me that our ego-based view of marriage is a fairly childish one, in which we see it simply as an outside thing in which, and from which, we have our every needs met and acquire happiness. While we maintain this simplistic, childish view of marriage and deny the mature and esoteric or inner view of marriage, we will go on being disappointed and fail to achieve what Jung terms a psychological relationship in which two consciously developed individuals relate by being able, in the first instance, to distinguish one's Self from the other.

OPPOSITE CONTAINMENT

As I already mentioned, in contemporary thinking, the issue of containment is not simply seen as being exclusively around the question of anima and animus. It seems to me, from my experience, more accurate to say that whatever is split-off from consciousness and forms as an opposite and major complex in the unconscious mind becomes the source of conflict between partners. Partners very often choose each other (unconsciously) as complements to express what they cannot express for themselves. So what one not uncommonly finds is a person who has an overdeveloped tendency to express emotions and feelings being attracted to and attractive to a person who is tight, rigid and unable to express any feelings. Now such a marriage will probably last and work quite well for some years, while both partners are able to ignore the unconscious factors that motivated them to choose each other in the first place. But, sooner or later, and usually the sooner, coming after ten or twelve years of marriage, the one who does all the emoting (the container), will start complaining about the rigidity and coldness of his or her partner (the contained), since their emotions are contained in their partner. Unconsciously, what this marriage is about is that the individual who experiences the intensity of her or his feelings may well have been reared in such a manner as to become fearful of the strength and intensity of her or his emotions, and therefore is attracted to a partner who is unconsciously perceived as strong, steadfast and able to control himself or herself, thus offering to protect the emotional partner from his or her own feelings, and hopefully to control those feelings.

Conversely rigid, controlling people choose as a mate someone who can do all the expressing of emotions for them, thereby relieving them of this struggle. These people more than likely were brought up in households where the expression of emotion was totally tabooed, and they are consciously unable to accept and express feelings in themselves. But, regretfully, feelings do not go away, so they choose a mate to do it for them, thus living vicariously off their emoting partner. The more emotional the partner becomes, the more satisfied they feel, on the one hand, and the more terrified, on the other, since it serves to remind them of their own unconscious feelings, which they are unable to accept.

Thus, in choosing a mate to express what they

cannot for themselves, such people at the same time find themselves disapproving of the very thing that they chose their partner for. The unconscious wish is often that, by attacking and controlling the unacceptable aspects they see and project onto somebody else, they can both attack and control those aspects within themselves. These sort of marriages are characterised by two halves, since half of each partner is projected onto the other. In Jung's terms there is no psychological relationship of any note in these relationships; on the contrary, it is of two half-unconscious components manifesting themselves in a relationship characterised by projection. In this sense the distinguishing between Self and other is very blurred.

A simple example of such a marriage is a couple who are now aged forty and thirty-eight, who have been married seventeen years and have two children, aged sixteen and fourteen. The husband admits that he chose his wife because of her delightful flamboyancy, sense of fun and light-heartedness. She says she chose him because he seemed so responsible and sensible. Both present clinically as now complaining exactly of these traits in each other. He says she is so inappropriate and unintellectual. She says he is so boring, stuffy, intellectually pretentious, too serious and always working everything out. She also says he has no fun. He was brought up to be the eldest responsible son in a traditionally religious family, in which success has been very important to him, in particular scholastic achievement. She, on the other hand, was brought up working class with a rejecting mother, no love, and an irresponsible father. She therefore chose a very responsible husband, whom she now complains about.

What has happened at mid-life in this marriage is that the man, after spending the first half of his life being a serious and very responsible person, firstly as a student and then subsequently in his profession, is now experiencing the unconscious stirrings of his repressed feminine side, and thus is complaining about his wife's inappropriateness and irresponsibility. In fact this is his attitude towards his own feminine side. It is he who needs to take back his playful, fun side from his wife and accept it as part of himself, instead of disapproving of it. She, at the same time, needs to accept some responsibility for her own life and not rely entirely on her husband in a projected form to the extent that she has. Both have unconsciously chosen a partner who contains their opposite or repressed side.

There it awaits reclamation, or redemption, a process that is awakened, I believe, by the arrival of mid-life, in which the opposite side stirs via the aegis of the anima or animus.

DEFENSIVE CONTAINMENT

I personally feel that the preceding sort of containment in a relationship has a better prognosis for the possibility of development of the two individuals than does another sort of containment, termed 'defensive containment'. In the preceding sort of containment, the partner is seen as containing the opposite aspects of oneself. In this second sort of containment, the defensive type of containment, it is the sameness that attracts each partner, and a denial of the opposites within themselves and between themselves. That is, both partners in this situation have the same unconscious fears, complexes, anxieties, and therefore choose each other in order to avoid situations they feel might create undue fear or anxiety. It is as if they form an unconscious agreement not to go near shared areas of anxiety. Thus, on the surface, these couples often appear very close, but unconsciously they are often poles apart, terrified of closeness and, in particular, of intimacy. They stick together consciously like glue, no separateness at all, no development of individual differences that may threaten separateness.

So, for example, one may find two people who suffer from a very low opinion of themselves attracted to each other on the basis of avoiding closeness, intimacy, so that they will not risk being hurt. Their marriage then is characterised by a lack of intimacy, which only has the effect of perpetuating lower self-esteem and feelings of worthlessness. An example of such a marriage is an intellectual couple both of whom were troubled throughout adolescence by guilt regarding their sexual feelings. The woman had previously been engaged to a boy whom she found exceedingly sexually exciting and attractive, but her mother had disapproved and she broke off the engagement and married her present husband. His father had died when he was thirteen and he felt very insecure as a male, particularly sexually, and chose his wife as he perceived her as 'a good girl'. Both wanted protection from their own sexual conflicts and sexual guilts. As a consequence of seeking this protection, they turned their marriage into a very workman-like agreement; both finished higher university degrees, they had two children, and were outwardly efficient, the ideal couple. Inwardly, they had absolutely no sexual relationship, no intimacy of any sort, and were actively avoiding any sexual behaviour that would generate further guilt. Then at forty years of age the husband fell in love with a young lady and left his wife. He was attracted to the young lady entirely on a physical basis, and complained that his wife was frigid. In this complaint he failed to remember that he chose her precisely because she was 'a good girl'.

MARRIAGE AND THE FOUR FUNCTIONS

Another way of thinking around this issue of containment, whether it be defensive or opposite containment, is to refer back to the concept of the four functions and personality types. Within this context the unconscious choice of partner that may be operating is the choice of a partner who has developed the opposite functions. So for example a very extroverted thinking/sensation type of male may choose an introverted intuitive/feeling type of female partner. Here the issue of opposites may remain buried or dormant for the first ten or twelve years of the marriage, then the onset of the mid-life transition will witness the evocation of conflict between the couple. In this situation the man's anima will inevitably be shaped by the inferior functions of intuition and feeling, and hence he will project his fear and contempt of these repressed qualities in himself onto his wife. It may manifest itself in such accusations as you are a 'predictable female, all intuition, where's your logic?' etc., etc. The female partner, on the other hand, will project her thinking and sensation function onto her husband and probably accuse him of 'always intellectualising, working things out in his head, always doing things and never discussing feelings', etc., etc. In such a marriage, what one can see beyond the more general aspect of anima and animus is that each partner is specifically containing the opposite functions for the other, and the eruption of anima and animus serves the psychological purpose of conveying these repressed functions into consciousness via projection, where work on them can begin.

However, where a marriage is characterised by partners having opposite functions in consciousness, and no shared or common function, often communication can be very difficult and the marriage characterised by prolonged periods of conflict. Each partner will tend to experience the feeling after, say, the initial period of the marriage, of having nothing in common and of feeling terribly misunderstood. What couples in these marriages often yearn for is a sense of sameness to counterbalance the differences generated from the opposites. Hence, not uncommonly, they will seek friendships outside the marriage, which are characterised by a high level of common interests. Such friendships, not uncommonly with the same sex, serve the purpose of providing the necessary sameness or balance to the sense of difference that so characterises the marriage.

The notion of sameness relates in another way to those marriages in which the partners have the same functions developed in unconsciousness. These marriages are those that were previously referred to as defensive containment marriages. Here, for example, the partners might be thinking/sensation types, having feeling and intuition in an inferior or repressed position. What has attracted each to the other, unconsciously, is the possibility of avoiding dealing with their inferior functions. If the opposite containment marriage is characterised by marked and obvious differences, these marriages are characterised by an equally obvious sameness or more euphemistically described as compatibility. For several years such a couple are viewed by outsiders as being an 'ideal couple'. They tend to do everything together, hold similar views and values, and generally exhibit a high degree of compatibility. However, the problem, somewhat ironically, lies in this very compatibility or sameness, because what these couples have great difficulty in managing is differences, whether such differences are in the realm of taste, attitudes, values or whatever. This difficulty stems from the fact that they find it difficult to tolerate differences, and tend to equate being different with conflict and badness. Hence such marriages in which the superior functions are similar tend to be free of any explicit conflict, and in fact they frequently avoid conflict. Hence outsiders are often shocked when such a seemingly ideal couple suddenly separate. The stimulus behind such separations is often the yearning not for sameness but for difference. Hence one not uncommon manifestation in such a marriage is extra-marital relationships, which generate some difference to counterbalance the sameness in the marriage. These marriages also seem not uncommonly to be negatively affected by the arrival of the first child. One explanation for this is simply that the child precipitates an awareness of differences, such as attitudes towards child-rearing and discipline. The child also, of course, upsets the previously organised unconscious arrangement between the couple.

There are obviously many possible combinations of either opposite or defensive containment. However, the central point is that with respect to the opposite type of marriage, what these couples lack is a shared language for communicating their differences. It is as if one person speaks French (for thinking/sensation) and the other German (feeling/intuition), but what they lack is a shared common language. Thus when conflict erupts, as it inevitably will in such relationships, it has the effect of polarising the individuals and propelling them farther into their superior functions, thereby accentuating the differences. For example, under tension the thinking type will become even more wordy and intellectual, and the feeling type more unable to express their thoughts and more emotional.

Likewise, the relationships characterised by sameness are unable to find a different language to express their differences, and become locked into habits and habitual ways of being together that prevent them from expressing differences. So, for example, if they both have the feeling and intuitive functions in an inferior position they tend to feel awkward and embarrassed about expressing feeling 'because that is something we don't do'. That is, they have no language that is different from the other and are therefore unable to foster or develop differences.

The most workable combination, in terms of the four functions and marriage or any relationship, is probably one in which one of the ego-conscious functions is shared. An example of this would be a couple in which one partner was superior thinking, with sensation as his or her auxiliary function and the other partner having feeling as the superior function with sensation the auxiliary. What appears to happen in such relationships is that when conflict erupts the couple at least have a bridge to each other through the sensation function. Thus they may avoid extreme polarisation and with sensation as the shared function perhaps find themselves both wanting to 'do' something as a way of initially dealing with the differences. It is as if the shared functions act as some sort of binding material against the threat of polarisation of differences. Such a couple as this would, of course, experience conflict around the shared inferior function of intuition, and they may both become frustrated with the absence of imagination and fantasy in the marriage. However, before they have to tackle this task, they may have built up some respect for differences through their shared auxiliary function and perhaps a method or mechanism for dealing with and facing conflict.

Another example of a workable relationship characterised by a shared function would be a relationship in which one partner was a thinking type with intuition the auxiliary function, and the other a feeling type with intuition the adjunct function. In this relationship the couple will presumably be able to be imaginative and intuitive in their attempts to deal with differences and also have the imaginative world through which they can communicate similarities. Thus the shared function arrangements provides a structure in which both similarities and differences can at least potentially be communicated and thus excessive polarisation or compatibility avoided. In this arrangement enough psychic energy will be available for the psychological work of withdrawing projections and at least theoretically the individuation process can continue.

Thus in our choice of partners we tend to get rid of those aspects we dislike in ourselves or find consciously unacceptable. The outer marriage becomes like the alchemist's vessel in which the essential ingredients for transformation into the internal marriage exist, but the danger is that we get stuck in the nigredo phase and are unable to take back our projections. That is a way of saying that we get caught in the blackness, get depressed because we are not happy. The contemporary Jungian viewpoint,* consistent with the alchemist's, is that marriage is not about happiness or well-being, but about salvation: that is, the redemption of our projected aspects, which we have placed onto our partner. This reclamation from the container of our split-off parts, the disowned and rejected aspects of our Self is the true salvation work. So marriage offers at one and the same time an immense opportunity for self-growth and maturation, and at the same time a powerful opportunity for total stagnation. The outcome is determined by whether we can grasp the esoteric aspects of marriage as well as the exoteric and find the necessary psychic energy for making the relationship conscious.

The alchemist's vessel, the *vas bene clausum,* the vessel in which the transformation took place, prior to the production of the philosopher's stone, is the marriage. This is Paracelsus's salt, which binds the mercury and sulphur. But, as we have discussed so often, the withdrawal of projection is extremely difficult. It is therefore not surprising that we have 'forgotten' the esoteric or inner aspects of marriage along with those

*See, for example, Adolf Guggenbuhl-Craig, *Marriage – Dead or Alive,* Spring Publications, 1977.

of alchemy, since to remember them, to see the outside marriage as the first step towards a true marriage to one's Self and the opposites within, would necessarily mean giving up blaming one's partner for one's own faults and accepting responsibility for one's Self. Then, instead of 'what is above is also below', we would also need to say that 'what is outside is also inside'.

9. Dreams and Symbols

The most consistent experience I have had in writing this book is how very difficult it is to get Jung's theoretical ideas into a coherent framework. Some chapters have been considerably easier to write than others, some much less taxing than others. However, in thinking about this chapter on dreams, I experienced my greatest difficulty. The very nature of psychology is subjective and cannot, in my view, be spoken or written about without doing some essential violence to its complexity.

Some of you will be aware that this book has moved from an outside spot to an increasingly inside one: from information about Jung the person, archetypes, Self, etc., all on the outside or periphery of one's immediate personal experience, to have perceptibly moved to personal and inside areas, such as anima and animus, and more specifically marriage. This chapter can be seen as epitomising the progressive movement inwards. Thus it is inevitable that I should experience it as the most difficult to write. There is a very wide gulf for me between the practitioner and the writer. If psychotherapeutic practice teaches one nothing else, it confirms again and again the uniqueness of each individual. The very nature of books is to provide general statement; for me this is very difficult to do, since no sooner have I written something than I can think of an instance that contradicts the rule stated in the written word.

Yet one is stuck with the conflict that people do wish

to know about themselves, and books on psychology are one step in that process. There is, in my opinion, an increasing urgency to know about oneself, to construct some sense of personal meaning as an antidote against what is experienced as an ever-increasing situation of meaninglessness.

Yet the yearning for that meaning is a complex matter, since on the one hand the fact that such a yearning exists reflects in part, I believe, the highly inflated position of rational thinking in our post-industrial, highly technologised society. In elevating thinking to such a superior position, and transforming science into a god, we have lost contact with our own earth, with the source and rhythm of our being, lost in a sense our place in the stream of things. This loss is experienced as a loss of meaning, a dis-ease of meaning. Hence the sense of urgency to correct the situation. Paradoxically our hope in many instances is that we can obtain it, or attain it, by the very same means by which we lost it; that is, through rational thinking. The unconscious hope, and in fact in many instances the conscious hope, in reading books on psychology is that additional information will magically provide the solution to one's inner chaos. In stating this I immediately suspect that some of you will deny that and *rationally* by saying to yourselves, 'No, that's not true; I would not be as childish or as simplistic as to expect to get answers.'

But such thoughts would represent the perpetuation of the rational mode, since my guess is that very few, if any, people would consciously expect answers or hold such a simplistic opinion. However, hopefully by now it has been established that much of our behaviour and attitudes are formed from our unconscious mind, that realm of psyche of which we have little or no awareness. Apropos of this, my further hunch is that many readers will approach this chapter with the specific hope that it will provide some sort of clear and concise information concerning the meaning of dreams. Some sort of hope that it will assert that 'if you dream of a black cat then . . .' etc.

This is what I would term the hope of literality. The hope that finally I would simply come clean and explain what's what, so that you can get on with your life and growth! Well, I regret to say that such an approach is utterly impossible and well it should be. Since the expectation that some recipe of symbols can be provided, which you can consult in order to understand your dreams and your own psyche, is for me the final absurdity of the technological, rational, literal perspective of our present day and age. The final absurdity of the hope that information and facts can alter how you feel about Self. Jung himself, as long ago as the late 1920s, spoke in a similar vein about such an approach when discussing dream interpretation. He said:

> More is required than routine recipes such as I have found in vulgar little dream books . . . Stereotyped interpretation of dream motifs is to be avoided; the only justifiable interpretations are those reached through a painstaking examination of the context [i.e. the individual context of the dream]. Even if one has great experience in these matters, one is again and again obliged, before each dream, to admit one's ignorance and renounce all preconceived ideas, to pre-

pare for something entirely unexpected.*

Here then lies the conflict in writing a chapter on dreams, a task that almost by its very nature demands stereotyped meanings. To me it is particularly interesting to note the two stereotyped attitudes prevailing towards dreams. On the one hand, there is the attitude that the meaning of dreams is straightforward and simply requires somebody with a knowledge of dreams to tell you what it means: a sort of childish hope for the magical answer. On the other hand, there exists an attitude that totally denies the validity of dreams and describes them as 'utter nonsense', 'rubbish', 'senseless stuff'. Both attitudes reflect, I believe, a defensive posture towards the unconscious mind. One wants to over-idealise it, see it as being all-meaningful and the source of truth, albeit simplistically. The other attitude is simply one of straightout denial. If I dared to generalise, I would say that it has been my impression that women tend to over-idealise dreams and hold them as the source of all meaning, and men tend to denigrate and deny the dream world. Both of these attitudes reflect, I believe, the respective attitudes towards the inner world. The workable position is probably to strive for a working relationship with the dream world, since in doing this one is striving and working towards a workable and harmonious relationship between the two aspects of our psyche, the conscious and the unconscious.

DREAM DEFINED

Having said all that, what then is a dream? According to Jung:

*'On the Nature of Dreams', in *CW* 8:286-7.

Dreams are impartial, spontaneous products of the unconscious psyche, outside the control of will. They are pure nature, they show us the unvarnished, natural fruit, and are therefore fitted, as nothing else is, to give us back an attitude that accords with our basic human nature when our consciousness has strayed too far from its foundations and run into an impasse.*

In another place Jung asserts:

The dream is specifically the utterance of the unconscious mind. Just as the psyche has a diurnal side which we call consciousness, so also it has a nocturnal side, the unconscious psychic activity, which we apprehend as dreamlike fantasy.†

Or

The dream shows the inner truth and the reality of the patient as it really is; not as I conjecture it to be, and not as he would like it to be, but as it is. (*CW* 16:304)

What each of these definitions brings out is that the dream and dreaming are essentially connected to the unconscious mind, both as an activity of that aspect of mind and indeed as proof of its very existence. Dreaming is a psychic phenomenon, which offers easy access to the contents of the unconscious mind. Indeed, Sigmund Freud described dreams as the *via regia,* the royal road, to the unconscious mind. However, be-

*'Meaning of Psychology for Modern Man', *CW* 10:317.
†'Practical Use of Dream Analysis', *CW* 16:317.

yond this assertion there would appear to be major disagreements and differences between Freud's and Jung's views on dreams. These differences cluster around two or three fundamental issues, which I think are well worth discussing, because in doing so one can hopefully gain a clearer idea of the Jungian view of dreams. These issues are:

1. Different use of the term 'symbol'.
2. Different view of the purpose of dreams (that is, whether retrospective or prospective).
3. Different views of the underlying psychic mechanism of dreams and dreaming.

The first distinction introduces the concept of a symbol as opposed to a sign. According to Jung, Freud meant sign when he said symbol, since a sign according to Jung is:

> Always less than the thing it points to; a symbol is always more than we understand at first sight. [Therefore] We never stop at the sign but go on to the goal it indicates; but we remain with the symbol because it promises more than it reveals.*

Herein lies the basic distinction. For Freud, a symbol, as he called it, disguised and concealed the true meaning. That is, a dream symbol really stood for something else; that is, it is less than it points to and within the Freudian framework dreams and their symbols (or signs) are disguised representations of a repressed wish (more often than not sexual and aggressive wishes). Therefore, the function of dreams in a Freudian sense is strictly one of wish-fulfilment.

**The Symbolic Life*, volume 18 of *CW*, p.212.

Technically this concealing quality of dreams is referred to as the distinction between the manifest and latent content. Perhaps an analogy would make this distinction clearer: that is, the distinction between Freud's use of symbols as merely a disguised representation of an unconscious wish, and Jung's use of symbols as the best possible statement of something that is not yet known and therefore would not be stated in any coherent or rational form. The analogy is that if Freud and Jung came upon an inscribed stone memorial in the desert, Freud would assume that it was a disguised version of a consciously known language such as English or German. Jung, on the other hand, would approach it as an archaeologist; it has meaning, but because it is in an unknown language the meaning must be sought.

Thus, for Freud, themes – or symbols as he called them in dreams – stood for other things, so a tree, for example, would stand for a penis, a cave for a vagina, etc. Thus for Freud an interpretation of a dream meant reducing the dream back to its basic meaning and uncovering the disguised and concealed meaning. However, Jung totally disagreed with this notion that dreams concealed things, since in his view, the symbolic view, the nature of dream images or symbols is to provide the most adequate representation of the state of mind at the time, its self-portrait, no more and no less. The Freudian view of concealment and disguise of an unconscious wish fits entirely and is entirely consistent with the Freudian notion of the personal unconscious, consisting of repressed and unacceptable wishes and feelings from consciousness. For Jung, as we have already seen, the unconscious is more than this, and indeed is also comprised of material that has never been conscious. On the notion of concealment of meaning, Jung had this to say:

> Since I have no reason to believe that the unconscious has any intention of concealing things, I must be careful not to project such a device onto its activity. It is characteristic of dreams to present pictorial and picturesque language to colourless and merely rational statements. This is certainly not an intentional concealment; it simply emphasises our inability to understand the emotionally charged picture language of dreams. (*CW* 18:204)

Well, if dreams are not about wish fulfilment of consciously unacceptable needs that have been repressed, and therefore have to be disguised, and thus their true meaning concealed from consciousness because it would be unacceptable and, furthermore, if dreams are not Freudian dreams, then what are they? It is in this connection that we return to the familiar theme of compensation and the nature of opposites. Jung states: 'There is no rule, let alone a law of dream interpretation, although it does look as if the general purpose of a dream is compensation' (*CW* 18:220). In other words, the tendency to compensate, or balance, or counteract a conscious attitude is an important characteristic of dreams, and indeed, according to Jung, must always be taken into account when attempting to understand a dream.

For Jung this compensatory or balancing quality of dreams had its equivalent in the nature of biological processes, where various reflexes maintained the internal state of the body within narrow ranges of temperature, oxygen, tension, blood pressure, etc., etc. For example, a person who restricts his own horizons in life because of an unhealthy and neurotic comparison with the achievements of his father, feels he would never be as good, etc., may actually dream of his father as being worse than he really is as a way of compensating for the conscious attitude of seeing him better than he actually is. Compensation is normally aimed at establishing some sort of psychological balance, and in this sense is a sort of self-regulating system operating between consciousness and the unconscious. Thus what one is attentive to in dreams is what conscious attitude might be being balanced or compensated for in the actual dream. So a person, for example, having an unduly favourable conscious view of herself or himself may dream of a most undesirable character in his or her dream. It also works the other way around. For example, if we habitually undervalue somebody, we are likely to have a highly flattering dream about that person, seeing her or him in a much higher position for example than he or she might normally occupy. This can, of course, be referring to some shadow aspect of ourselves, or perhaps anima or the animus that we have consciously denigrated and placed into a lowly valued position. So, in essence, the compensatory mechanism operates in such a way that it often takes the opposite view to consciousness, where that conscious view has got to a lopsided spot. If, on the contrary, the conscious attitude is 'correct', then the dreams may have the function of pointing the way to further growth, individuation. This compensatory nature of dreams relates to the additional issue of the differences between Freud and Jung, since in the Jungian framework dreams are not only about the past (retrospective), but also about the future (prospective). Obviously from a Freudian viewpoint, if dreams are wish-fulfilments, then they tend to refer to material from the past, usually from childhood, which has been repressed out of consciousness. But because Jung has the compensatory viewpoint, the dreams can be seen as correcting something in the present and pointing to needed changes in the future in order to balance the psyche. On this point Jung says:

Considering a dream from the standpoint of finality which I contrast with the causal standpoint of Freud, does not – as I would expressly like to emphasise – involve a denial of the dream's causes, but rather a different interpretation of the associative material gathered around the dream. The material facts remain the same but the criterion by which they are judged is different. The question may be formulated simply as follows: What is the purpose of this dream? What effect is it meant to have?*

One of the points at which this finality, as Jung calls it, or prospective purposeful future orientative quality of dream shows up is in the initial dreams that an individual may bring to psychotherapy; that is, the dream she or he has just before his or her first appointment. That she or he would have such a dream ought not be surprising, since presumably one goes to sleep thinking of the meeting with this stranger tomorrow and wondering what sort of things will be talked about.

*'General Aspects of Dream Psychology', *CW* 8:243.

The following dreams, of three patients, all amply demonstrate this quality of the dream to be both retrospective and prospective. They are also of an invaluable help in the initial stage of psychotherapy, because they both point to what has been a problem, been the cause of the problem and often give a clue as to what direction to proceed.

The first patient was a twenty-two-year-old single girl, whose presenting problem was one of depression, which had come to the fore during a recent holiday. She in fact had this dream some time before she saw me, and it was this dream that, she said, had prompted her to contact me. The dream was as follows:

I was with my mother visiting a close family at a girlfriend's house and had stayed overnight and was sick in the morning. My mother was to drive me to work and I was very concerned about being late. We were driving down High Street looking across to the right and there was a friend of mine and three other young people in a car moving at the same pace slightly ahead of us. I had a very strong desire to be in this other car with my friend but was held back in my mother's car. I was late for work and I missed my first appointment with a colleague and I had a strong sense of not living up to my responsibilities, of having let my colleague down and also of being very, very angry with my mother.

This dream, to my mind, clearly demonstrates the problem: that is, the girl travelling down a main road in her mother's car unable to join her peer group. In other words, this patient's problem was of having to learn some separateness between herself and her mother and, indeed, as it turned out, this was precisely the problem. The dream also indicates that the direction in which she should head is towards developing ordinary heterosexual relationships with people of her own age. She was able to share with me that one of the reasons she had not developed any separateness from her mother was an over-riding fear that if she did, her mother would get sick and possibly die.

The second patient was a thirty-eight-year-old woman, married, with three children, who also presented with underlying feelings of depression and despair, coupled with some confusion. These were the result of a recent extra-marital affair she had had before returning to her marriage of some fifteen years' duration. The dream was as follows:

I was in a schoolroom building of some sort with two of my children and some boys came into the room and were skylarking around with matches. I became very concerned because I was aware that there was petrol around somewhere in the room. I tried to tell the boys to put the matches away – it was dangerous. They did not and suddenly a fire started. One of my daughters threw herself on the fire with the intent of putting it out. I pulled her off and she was badly burnt, mainly on the underside of her arms.

This person also had a second dream prior to her initial visit with me. The second dream was implying the scene of falling, grabbing onto something and a deep, deep, dark pit. She also had a third dream in the sequence, which is not unusual, and this one again I think is important.

Her daughters had been staying in the city and her husband had gone to pick them up. One of the daughters did not want to come home, so they left her in the city and came home with the other. When they arrived home panic set in and they went back to get the daughter they left behind but couldn't find her.

These three dreams relate to this woman's problem, which was that for the entire period of her married life and indeed some years before, she had decided to live on the outside of herself, presenting a happy, coping and controlled persona to the outside world. With the advent of mid-life this persona had been disturbed and disrupted by the eruption of the animus function in this woman. The dream dates very precisely in my mind that the problem started at about thirteen years of age, because this was the age of the daughter who had thrown herself on the fire and burnt the underneath of her arms. So the first segment of the dream then points to the diagnostic or retrospective quality, the dream indicating that the difficulties in this woman's life started at around thirteen years of age. Symbolically one could see the boys who are threatening to ignite the fire as being the undifferentiated animus or masculine parts of this woman, threatening to ignite her sexual and aggressive feelings. This, of course, is precisely what had been ignited with the onset of the mid-life crisis.

Her second dream indicates some of the fear of falling and trying to hold onto a conscious viewpoint, but the fear that there was a deep, deep pit perhaps is suggestive of the fear of her unconscious mind. Her third dream further confirms the first initial dream by pointing to the fact that she had left one of her daughters behind in Melbourne and went back and couldn't find her. This daughter, according to the woman, was very much like herself, whereas the one that she had brought home was like the Self that had been operative in the first half of her life. So again all three dreams point to the work that needs to be done and actually dates the spot at which the problem first started in this particular person.

The third patient was a forty-nine-year-old man, recently separated for the second time. Whilst this dream was not technically produced prior to the first meeting, it was produced by the unconscious mind immediately following the first meeting, and hence has the same quality, I believe, of an initial dream. This man's problem was that he was feeling confused and uncertain about himself and his feelings as the result of the failure of his second marriage. As he was employed in the helping professions, he was very concerned that he should be able to understand himself and the meaning of this for his own work. The man concerned had also been unaware of his own dreams for some years and was quite surprised when he produced this dream. Here is the dream:

I was passing through a series of underground caverns on some sort of sightseeing tour. There was a lot of jocular exchanges as if we were teenagers. A young woman placed herself in my arms with me standing behind her. In spite of my puzzled feeling and reluctance she pulled me into a warmer, closer physical contact with her and seemed to be very affectionate and enjoying the contact. I was puzzled but enjoyed the contact myself. A young man, perhaps her brother, was looking at us very askance and there seemed to be an impression that she belonged to another.

The scene then changed and I found myself in an elevated position looking down on a sloping back yard. There were a series of pitheads indicating where the underground caverns were that I had just been through.

The scene changed again. This time I found myself in a series of underground bunkers in the jungle hiding from the Japanese (knew this, although I couldn't see it). Women in tattered clothing emerged from the jungle into a clearing. They began setting up camp on the surface above our hidden bunker. I knew that that would give away our position and I asked one of them 'You're not going to camp there are you?' The women paid no heed. One woman carried a centipede-like creature and arose to withdraw into the jungle to cook and eat it. Another woman had a mouse-like creature with an elongated body and a mouse's head. She laid it on the ground and took out a two-pronged meat fork (the one in my kitchen!) and plunged it repeatedly into the body of this creature. It accepted this without pain, protest or a struggle. I knew somewhere that it had to be sacrificed for food but it wasn't dying. The fork then passed through the creature's head pinning it to the ground. It accepted this with only a mild flinch of the eyes. I found myself watching with a mixture of horror and fascination. Then I seemed to lose consciousness as the creature died. I awoke with surprise that I had been asleep. That was a dream!

Whilst there are many, many things contained in this dream, the one consistent theme is the contact with the feminine side of himself as exemplified in the first segment of being a teenager and in the third segment in which he finds himself underground with the women above him. The first segment again points to a teenage level of development, and one could speculate from this dream that the loss of contact with a feminine soul happened somewhere around the early teenage years, because he has a feeling that she 'belonged to another'. The second scene, to my mind, indicates when he is looking down from an elevated position at the series of pitheads that in fact this is the over-development of his rational thinking side, which is now looking down at the inferior side still buried in the unconscious. The third scene, hiding from the Japanese, tends to indicate hiding from his own unconscious, since that would personify foreign parts of himself. The women in tattered clothing emerging from the jungle could perhaps be seen as the anima emerging from the jungle into the clearing. The fork going through the elongated mouse creature can, I believe, be seen symbolically as the necessary suffering and pain having to be inflicted in order to disturb and temporarily waylay his rational functioning in order to allow this man to make contact with his feminine Self. The outer world situation of this man would tend to confirm the fact that he had great problems with his anima, which was the conveyor of the feeling of his personality. Such problems could be seen to be related to his outer world marital difficulties resulting in two separations.

Whilst one could say a great deal here about each of these dreams, I think what is important is that we now turn to the attitude that one ought to have towards dreams and interpretations of them.

ATTITUDE TOWARDS DREAMS AND INTERPRETATION

Jung once said that it is so difficult to understand a dream that for a long time he made a rule: 'When someone tells me a dream and asks for my opinion, to say first of all to myself "I have no idea what this dream means", after that I can begin to examine the dream' (*CW* 8:533).

In the Tavistock lectures Jung continues this theme by stating: 'I always welcome that feeling of incompetence because then I know I shall put some good work into my attempt to understand the dream.'*

We could all take a leaf out of Jung's book as a necessary corrective to our rational conscious impatience to understand a dream immediately and 'get it right'. How, then, does Jung handle or interpret a dream? His approach is termed amplification and is different from the Freudian approach, which is called free association. In Jung's words, his attitudes towards working on a dream are as follows: 'I want to know what the dream is. Therefore, I handle the dream as if it were a text which I do not understand properly, say a Latin, Greek or Sanskrit text.'†

**Analytical Psychology*, p. 92.
†Ibid.

The dream, as we have already discussed from a Jungian point of view, is not about concealment, but certainly needs deciphering in the same way as an ancient text does. This approach Jung termed amplification. That is, exploring and finding the context of each of the main symbols in the dream by simply asking the question, 'What might this or that in the dream mean to me?' As far as possible, one explores each image or symbol and tries to grasp its particular and specific meaning for that particular and specific person. One asks the question 'What strikes you as significant about that particular piece of a dream?' 'What is the atmosphere of the dream?' 'What mood did you have upon waking?' By amplifying, a dreamer can come to see the dream in the setting of other events in her or his life. Such amplification is carried out consciously and usually by sticking very closely to the dream images themselves. By contrast, the Freudian idea of free association is simply encouraging the dreamer to state whatever comes to his or her mind in connection with the dream. Jung felt that 'free association' led away from the dream. For example, if somebody dreamed of a table, the association might be to a writing desk, whereas Jung points out that he will keep returning to the specific image of that specific table and ask the patient what that table means to him. That is, in Jung's terms you explore what connection or meaning the particular table has.

Jung says that when the context of each dream has been established then one can venture an interpretation of its meaning. This establishing of the individual context of a dream is often very painstaking work, and one dream can occupy the best part of a normal hour's consultation. When we come to interpreting a dream, another way to think of it, according to Jung, is to think of a dream as if it were an ancient Greek play with four distinct phases:

1. Place, time and personnel: exposition phase.
2. Exposition and statement of the problem: development of plot.
3. Culmination, something happens: peripeteia.
4. Solution: lysis. (*CW* 8:294-5)

However, even more useful, I believe, than this particular approach, ableit this being valuable in itself, and even more productive than immediately worrying about amplification is, I think, the overall conscious attitude we adopt towards the dream and the dream world, since this attitude will be the attitude we have towards our inner world in general. James Hillman, a brilliant contemporary Jungian, offers a superbly simple idea in relation to this issue of the attitude one should take towards a dream. He simply asserts that we should 'befriend the dream'. This, according to Hillman, means:

To participate in it, to enter into its imagery and mode, to want to know more about it, to understand, play with, carry and become familiar with, as one would do with a friend . . . As I grow familiar with my dreams I grow familiar with my inner world. Who lives in me? What inscapes are mine? What is recurrent and therefore keeps coming back to reside in me?*

For Hillman the issue with dreams is not rational dream interpretation, which he sees as often turning

*James Hillman, *Insearch*, Spring Publications, 1979, p. 57.

into a wanting from the unconscious, using it to gain information, power, energy, and generally exploiting it for the sake of the ego. No! For Hillman the dream offers the opportunity for healing a split house within ourselves: the house that is split between consciousness and unconsciousness.

Therefore what counts most is the relation to the dream itself. This stems in large part from the conscious attitude that we hold towards the dream and dream world. Hence, for Hillman, as in a friendship the first step is a non-interpretative approach, giving the dream time and being patient with it, not jumping to conclusions. Befriending simply means taking time to listen, as indeed one would in the beginning of any friendship. In other words, we must allow the dream to speak for itself, rather than pursuing it with intellectual analysis. Part of 'letting it speak for itself' is the amplificatory process, letting the meaning roll around or, in Hillman's terms, 'let the dream tell its own story', and by so doing become our own mythologist, which originally means 'teller of tales'. For Hillman it is through this attitude of befriending and listening to the dream that we affirm the value of our Soul (Self) and give due recognition to this aspect of being.

Jung says something very similar about paying attention to dreams when he says:

To concern ourselves with dreams is a way of reflecting on ourselves – a way of self-reflection. It is not our ego-consciousness reflecting on itself; rather, it turns its attention to the objective actuality of the dream as a communication or message from the unconscious, unitary Soul of humanity. It reflects *not* the ego, but on the *Self.**

A connecting link throughout this book has been that each of us needs to discover our personal myth or myths and to engage in this process, which has been termed Soul-making or Self-making. Listening and recognising our dreams is a Soul-making activity, readily available to all of us, which enhances the movement forward of the individuation process, both for the individual and for mankind.

*'The Meaning of Psychology for Modern Man', *CW* 10:149.

10. Conclusion

In the Preface to this book I asserted that it was an introduction to Jung, and that it will have failed as a book if it did not leave the reader with a desire to explore Jung in greater detail and depth. Hence, to write a Conclusion as such is inappropriate and also inconsistent with the nature of the material and issues discussed in this book. There really can be no conclusion to these issues, just an ongoing commitment to the process of individuation and the evolution of consciousness. To yearn for a conclusion or to feel the need to write one is to belong to that ego realm of mind that seeks clarity and non-ambiguity, the level of mind that is comfortable and contented with simplistic linear thinking 'if this, then that'. Well, as Jung once said, 'Non-ambiguity and non-contradiction are one sided and thus unsuited to express the incomprehensible.'* Thus I can think of no better way to 'conclude' this book than by re-quoting the words of Eliot from 'Little Gidding':

> What we call the beginning is often the end
> And to make an end is to make a beginning
> The end is where we start from.

*'Introduction to the Religious and Psychological Problems of Alchemy', *CW* 12:15.

Suggestions for Further Reading

JUNG'S LIFE

Vincent Brome, *Jung: man and myth*, Granada, 1978

Barbara Hannah, *Jung: his life and work*, Michael Joseph, 1977

Aniela Jaffé, *From the Life and Work of C.G. Jung*, Harper & Row, 1971

C. G. Jung, *Memories, Dreams and Reflections*, Routledge & Kegan Paul, 1963

Laurens van der Post, *Jung and the Story of our Time*, Vintage Books, 1977

Marie-Louise von Franz, *Carl Gustav Jung: his myth in our time*, Little Brown & Co., 1975

JUNGIAN THEORY

E. A. Bennett, *What Jung Really Said*, Schocken Books, 1966

Frieda Fordham, *An Introduction to Jung's Psychology*, Pelican, 1953

Calvin S. Hall and Vernon J. Nordby, *A Primer of Jungian Psychology*, Mentor Books, 1973

Jolande Jacobi, *The Psychology of C. G. Jung*, Routledge & Kegan Paul, 1962

C. G. Jung et al., *Man and his Symbols*, Doubleday/Alders Books, 1964

Anthony Storr, *Jung*, edited by F. Kermode, Fontana Modern Masters Series, 1973

Anthony Storr (ed.), *Jung: selected writings*, Fontana, 1983

Edward C. Whitmont, *The Symbolic Quest*, Princeton University Press, 1978

APPLICATIONS OF JUNG'S THEORIES

Liz Greene, *Relating: an astrological guide to living with others on a small planet*, Coventure, 1977

James A. Hall, *Jungian Dream Interpretation: a handbook of theory and practice*, Inner City Books, 1983

Esther Harding, *The Way of All Women*, David McKay, 1933/1961

The I and the Not I: a study in the development of consciousness, Princeton University Press, 1965

Women's Mysteries, Ancient and Modern, Putnam's, 1971

Psychic Energy: its source and its transformation, Princeton/Bollingen Paperback, 1973

Robert A. Johnson, *He: understanding masculine psychology*, Harper & Row, 1977

She: understanding feminine psychology, Harper & Row, 1977

P. W. Martin, *Experiment in Depth*, Routledge & Kegan Paul, 1955

Peter O'Connor, *Understanding the Mid-life Crisis*, Sun Books, 1981

Sylvia Perera, *Descent to the Goddess: a way of initiation for women*, Inner City Books, 1980

John A. Sanford, *Dreams and Healing*, Paulist Press, 1978

The Invisible Partners, Paulist Press, 1980

Marie-Louise von Franz, *The Feminine in Fairytales*, Spring Publications, 1972

Interpretation of Fairytales, Spring Publications, 1978

Alchemy: an introduction to the symbolism and the psychology, Inner City Books, 1980

Edward C. Whitmont, *Return of the Goddess: femininity, aggression and the modern grail quest* Routledge & Kegan Paul, 1983

Frances G. Wickes, *The Inner World of Choice*, Prentice-Hall, 1963

Marion Woodman, *The Owl was a Baker's Daughter: obesity, anorexia nervosa and the repressed feminine*, Inner City Books, 1980

THE COLLECTED WORKS OF C. G. JUNG

C. G. Jung, *Collected Works*, edited by Sir Herbert Read, Michael Fordham, Gerhard Adler and William McGuire. Translated by R. F. C. Hull (except for volume 2). Princeton: Princeton University Press (Bollingen Series XX); London: Routledge & Kegan Paul.

1. *Psychiatric Studies*, 1957
2. *Experimental Researches* (translated by L. Stein in collaboration with Diana Riviere), 1973
3. *The Psychogenesis of Mental Disease*, 1960
4. *Freud and Psychoanalysis*, 1961
5. *Symbols of Transformation*, 2nd ed. 1967
6. *Psychological Types*, 1971
7. *Two Essays on Analytical Psychology*, 2nd ed. 1966
8. *The Structure and Dynamics of the Psyche*, 2nd ed. 1969
9. Part 1. *The Archetypes and the Collective Unconscious*, 2nd ed. 1968
   Part 2. *Aion: researches into the phenomenology of the Self*, 2nd ed. 1968
10. *Civilization in Transition*, 1964
11. *Psychology and Religion: West and East*, 2nd ed. 1969

12. *Psychology and Alchemy*, 2nd ed. 1968
13. *Alchemical Studies*, 1967
14. *Mysterium Coniunctionis: an inquiry into the separation and synthesis of psychic opposites in alchemy*, 2nd ed. 1970
15. *The Spirit in Man, Art and Literature*, 1966
16. *The Practice of Psychotherapy*, 2nd ed. 1966
17. *The Development of Personality*, 1954
18. *The Symbolic Life: miscellaneous writings*, 1975
19. *General Bibliography of C. G. Jung's writings*, 1979
20. *General Index to the Collected Works of C. G. Jung*, 1979

Index